MW01295013

Quitting Weed: The Complete Guide
© Matthew Clarke 2018
All rights reserved
ISBN: 9781976799846

This book is designed to provide information and motivation to readers. It is sold with the understanding that its contents do not constitute a type of psychological, legal, or any other kind of professional advice. The author shall not be liable for any physical, psychological, emotional, financial, or commercial damages, including, but not limited to, special, incidental, consequential, or other damages. You are responsible for your own choices, actions, and results. Every individual's addiction and quitting experience is different.

Political Disclaimer

Naturally, in a free and open society, adults have the right to choose what to put into their bodies. Prohibition is unquestionably harmful to both society and the individual. None of these things are in dispute.

Having said that, some people find their cannabis use problematic. For those who are unable (not through want of trying) to moderate their habit, then complete abstinence is the only sensible course of action. It is for these people that this book is written.

Just as there are responsible drinkers and alcoholics, there are those who can moderate their weed use and those who cannot. It is not that alcohol or weed is inherently harmful, but some people are unable to use it responsibly.

This book is not anti-cannabis: it is anti-cannabis abuse. For most people, casual cannabis use does not interfere with their lives in any significant way. Most are able to use cannabis responsibly – others, however, cannot.

If you can smoke weed and not have it cause any problems for you, good for you. Just because you can moderate your use, that doesn't mean everyone else can.

Seeking help and advice on trying to quit any addiction is a good thing. This book is not demonising the drug itself, rather the effects it has when used excessively. That is what this book is about. It is a simple recognition that some people find regulating their cannabis intake difficult – just as others do with alcohol.

Table of Contents

<u>Introduction</u>

About the Author

This book was written to help those who are struggling to quit cannabis, as well as to help me overcome my own addiction. My own quitting process involved three years of cutting down, stopping, starting, stopping, repeatedly relapsing, before finally stopping for good. This book is a result of my research and my journey of self-discovery that enabled me to be able to quit for good.

It took me a long time to quit. Having heavily used cannabis between the ages of 16 and 29 (all day, every day for most of those years), it was a huge part of my identity. It gradually occurred to me that my heavy cannabis use may have been holding me back in life. I began to question my use, eventually realising that my perpetual underachievement and refusal to grow up and face responsibilities was firmly linked to my weed habit.

This was a startling thought since I had never properly questioned my cannabis use. I had unquestioningly regarded it as a good thing, never stopping to honestly reflect on its role in my life. Unaware, I simply cocooned myself away, smoking away my troubles and avoiding my problems.

I had long been in denial of my addiction. I eventually realised that I was abusing the substance, using it to escape my responsibilities and emotions, and using it to fill unmet needs. That realisation marked the beginning of my quitting journey.

Given my long history of cannabis abuse, and the length of time it took me to successfully quit, I am testament to the fact that anyone can achieve cannabis sobriety.

Who This Book Is For

This book is for those who are tired of the negative impact cannabis has on their lives. It is for people who are conscious of the effect weed has on their lives, yet struggle to leave it behind, perhaps feeling overwhelmed by the obstacles.

This book is intended to be a powerful, comprehensive tool for helping you to break free of cannabis addiction. It is focused on understanding your habit, understanding what is holding you back, understanding the obstacles you are going to face, and understanding how to overcome them. It is a complete look at the process of quitting, aimed at equipping you with the knowledge and awareness to help you quit cannabis for good – leaving your hazy, smoke-filled days of regret behind you.

Quitting cannabis is not the easiest thing to do, and many find themselves unable to shake off their habit despite the strongest of intentions. Unlike other books on the subject, it will never be claimed to be "easy" – if it were that easy to quit, there wouldn't be a problem in the first place.

Whilst I do not promise it is easy, I do promise that it is *possible*. With this book, and your determination, you can beat your addiction and start living the life you seek.

Whether you are just starting to consider quitting, or whether you are in the middle of trying to quit, this book offers knowledge and practical advice to help you overcome your dependency on cannabis.

What Is in This Book

Many of us fail to overcome our addiction because we do not have a concrete plan, a deep enough understanding of the recovery process, or a deep enough understanding of ourselves and the role cannabis plays in our lives. It is with these things in mind that this book is written.

We will begin by putting cannabis addiction in perspective, before assessing the consequences of our use. Then, we will look at the science of cannabis and its impact on the mind and body, followed by an exploration of the psychological motives behind our use – understanding the exact role it occupies in our lives and the reasons why we are so compelled to abuse it.

With this secure foundation, we will then overview the journey ahead, before looking at strategies and tips for quitting successfully. We will then explore the obstacles to quitting, before learning about relapses and how to best avoid them.

Towards the end of the book, we will consider the "Quitting Mindset" – how to mentally approach the quitting process. The final chapter will detail the benefits of sobriety, as well as provide handy motivational thoughts for you to consider whenever the urge to smoke strikes. At the end of the book, there is an inspiring collection of quitting stories, to help encourage you to stay the course and to get perspective on the journey ahead.

Chapter 1: The Invisible Chains

"Addictions ... started out like magical pets, pocket monsters. They did extraordinary tricks, showed you things you hadn't seen, were fun. But came, through some gradual dire alchemy, to make decisions for you. Eventually, they were making your most crucial life-decisions. And they were ... less intelligent than goldfish."

William Gibson

The Sedated Life

You wake up, your head feels groggy. You have little energy. After forcing yourself to get up, within an hour, you have a smoke.

You slowly go about your day. Maybe you work, maybe you don't. Conversation is difficult; you are unable to look people in the eye, unable to even string a coherent sentence together. You feel ashamed over your impoverished social skills. You never laugh or smile anymore; you seem to be in a permanent state of numbness. All you are concerned about is looking towards the next high, even though each subsequent high of the day is less and less effective at making you feel ok.

Evening rolls around, and once again you find yourself in front of the TV or computer, numbing and distracting yourself further. You gorge yourself on take-away food and unhealthy snacks. Any tasks or jobs you had planned have been left for another day.

This terrible cycle continues day in, day out. You alternate between momentarily feeling good, before returning to that familiar state: lethargic, fuzzy, empty, numb, and above all, unhappy with life. Each day, you find that a little part of you dies; each day, you get slightly further away from your real self.

Sometimes, you wonder if there is another life out there, away from the weed, away from the lonely, monotonous existence that your life has become. For a brief moment, you stop pretending that life is all good, and you begin to gaze upon the reality you have been blinding yourself to: you have neglected your life.

You have traded in real growth and development in favour of a meaningless, artificial euphoria, kidding yourself that all is fine when the reality is anything but. As the discomfort of this truth starts to set in, your brain persuades you why you should continue to smoke: it helps open your mind, it's a social activity, it helps you be creative, it helps take the edge off the futility of life, it's harmless, everyone does it, it's not heroin, and so on, and so on.

You reach for your stash box once again.
There must be more to life than this.
There is.

The Reality of Cannabis Addiction

Cannabis addiction is a very real phenomenon, as the reader of this book will know. It may not be as obvious or as damaging as heroin or crack addiction; however, the damage is there, and it is easier to go unnoticed. Weed addiction can, to some degree, be concealed. You may have a steady job or a relationship, outwardly appearing to be "successful." As a result, cannabis addiction is shrouded in mystery, half-truths, and misinformation. Many deny that it even exists.

"You can't be addicted to weed – it's not heroin."
"It's not physically addictive – it's all in your head."
"It's your own fault if you keep smoking all day, every day, and never get anything done."

These comments completely misunderstand what addiction is and how it works. Just as there are responsible drinkers and alcoholics, there are responsible cannabis users and addicts.

Weed affects every individual differently. For some, after a certain period – a few months or a few years – the benefits of smoking no longer outweigh the negatives. When most people reach this point, they quietly drop the habit. Some people, however, find themselves unable to stop.

Those who claim it is not addictive tend to dispute the definition of addiction. Here's the thing: whether a substance is physically addictive or psychologically addictive is irrelevant – if using a substance is causing you significant trouble in your life, and you find it difficult to stop using it, you are addicted.

You know have a problem with your weed use if you identify with any of the following:

- You barely, if ever, go a day without getting high.
- You are irritable, anxious, or depressed without it.
- You are spending more than you can afford on it.

- You choose friends and relationships based on their level of cannabis use.
- You fail to attend to your day-to-day responsibilities.
- You find it difficult, or impossible, to cut down.
- Your weed use interferes with your work or school performance.

Cannabis Abuse in Perspective

Cannabis is the most widely used recreational drug in the world. Whilst most people use it responsibly, it is estimated that around 1 in 10 users fit the criteria for abuse or addiction, although that figure may be higher.

In the US, the total number of marijuana users is estimated at 19.8 million, meaning that around 2 million people meet the clinical criteria for marijuana dependency.

In the UK in 2011, 60,000 individuals sought cannabis addiction treatment, with only an estimated 1 in 10 addicts seeking out treatment in the first place.

In Australia, which has a relatively high number of cannabis users, 32,321 people sought treatment for cannabis addiction in 2011/12.

These statistics may be above or below the actual number; however, for our purposes, they illustrate an undeniable fact: millions of people worldwide cannot use cannabis responsibly. Given only a small fraction of those addicted seek professional help, there are clearly a lot of addicts out there. You are not alone in your struggle with the green herb.

The Slow Descent into Addiction

Cannabis addiction creeps up on you.

Getting high started out as the most amazing, wonderful thing. It was a cheap, fun, spiritual, rebellious, mind-expanding experience – with no hangover. Listening to music was mind-blowing; you had wonderfully expansive thoughts about life and the world; you had amazing experiences and conversations.

However, from that first day you smoked, little did you know, there was a time limit on how long it would be fun, before addiction set in.

What started as a bit of fun gradually turned into psychological dependency. Months and years soon drifted by in a smoke-filled haze. Cannabis use became so deeply entrenched in your life, you began to find it impossible to imagine life without it. When questioned about your use by a concerned friend or family member, you refused to admit there might be a problem. You said you could easily stop if you wanted to – a day that never came.

Then, one seemingly normal day, you asked yourself, "Is being high all the time actually a good thing?" The first few times you thought this, you brushed it aside and continued using. Eventually though, that niggling concern got louder and louder until one day you thought to yourself, "I might actually have a problem."

You begin to realise that you have neglected yourself – physically, emotionally, and spiritually. Your mind is slow and sluggish, you have difficulty concentrating, difficulty thinking clearly, and difficulty finding the motivation to get out of bed, let alone sort your life out. The path ahead is daunting.

Overcoming the Stigma of Addiction

The word "addiction" has such a massive cultural and social attachment to it that we automatically flinch upon hearing the word. However, for our own sake, we must overcome this negative stigma. It's time we own our situation, without shame.

At first, you may feel reluctant to assign yourself the label of "addict." We find this difficult because society has taught us that addicts are filthy, pathetic, desperate individuals devoid of morals, not worthy of sympathy or help. The first many times I thought I might be addicted, I thought I was exaggerating. When I told my friends, they also thought I was exaggerating. This, I realise now, was denial.

This denial is very powerful: if you think, "No, I'm not an addict," you are delaying your progress. The purpose of owning this label is about self-honesty, not self-hatred. An addict is not someone to be pitied or loathed; it is simply a description of an individual's unhealthy relationship to a substance.

After all, weed is simply one of many ways to self-medicate. Where others are addicted to work, shopping, the internet, sex, pornography, or hoarding animals, we happen to find comfort in the numbing and therapeutic effects of a particular psychoactive drug.

As cliché as it is, admitting is the first step. Giving yourself the title of "addict" is actually quite liberating. It is not a judgemental title, just an accurate one. Acknowledging our "addiction" for what it is gets us in the right mindset for change.

Conclusion

To overcome cannabis addiction, the first thing you must do is take responsibility. No one else is responsible for your addiction apart from you. No one else is going to rescue you from yourself – **you must take responsibility for your own life.**

For many of us, this can be extremely difficult. Some of us have an allergy to responsibility; everything that's wrong in our lives we blame on someone or something else – some external circumstance or situation, or something that happened to us in the past. This may make us feel better in the short term, but we end up giving up our power to do something about it.

Think about it: if we are not ultimately responsible for our actions – that our addiction is purely down to the troubles in our lives, the nature of the drug, or our genes – then we end up viewing ourselves as slaves to cannabis. Certainly, these factors are significant in *contributing* to our addiction; however, the danger is in blaming these things *entirely* for our situation. Whilst we should acknowledge the circumstances of our addiction, we must accept overall responsibility.

Chapter 2: Analysing Your Habit

"Everything you want in life has a price connected to it. There's a price to pay if you want to make things better, a price to pay just for leaving things as they are, a price for everything."

Harry Browne

Having become so de-sensitized to our use, many of us are not fully aware of the damage our addiction causes. When we honestly consider the true cost of our cannabis use, we strengthen our commitment to quitting.

This chapter will encourage you to open your eyes to the reality of your addiction and the impact it has on your life. Here, in black and white, we will consider what our habit *really* costs us – not just in terms of money, but everything else that we give up in the process.

To assess the impact cannabis has on our lives, we will first consider the **opportunity costs** of our use. Then, we will take an in-depth look at the **costs and "benefits"** of our weed use. At the end of the chapter, it should be clear just how devastating your habit truly is.

From this point on, we must be honest with ourselves: if we are going to be successful, we must be absolutely clear about the reality of our use. Just as buildings need foundations, we need strong foundations to build our sobriety upon. Denying or minimizing the reality of addiction risks the entire quitting process.

Opportunity Costs

An opportunity cost refers to the opportunities we lose when we choose one particular option over another.

When we have the choice between two or more things, *where we can only choose one,* picking one results in losing the ability to choose the other. This is an incredibly powerful concept. **By choosing to use cannabis, you close the door to other opportunities.**

- If you choose to smoke every day and eat lots of junk food, you lose the opportunity of being fit and healthy and all the benefits that would bring.

- If you choose to smoke every day, you lose energy and vigour. As a result, you get fewer things done, which erodes your confidence and self-esteem.

- If you choose to spend your evenings smoking with friends, you lose the opportunity of sitting at home reading a book, meeting new people, attending evening classes, or volunteering your time to a good cause – along with all the positive emotions and consequences of those activities.

- If you choose to spend most of your disposable income on weed, you lose the opportunity to save and gain financial security, or to spend that money on your loved ones, holidays, gifts, or whatever else you can't afford.

Cannabis Addiction: A Cost/Benefit Analysis

When thinking about your weed use, and the role it plays in your life, it is *really* useful to conduct a cost/benefit analysis. A detached assessment of your use – both the positives and negatives – will enable you to put your use into perspective.

We will divide our assessment into the benefits and costs of our use, considering both the short-term and long-term consequences. Please note, this is not a completely exhaustive list, and you may find that you don't identify with all of them. However, there will likely be a few points that really hit home. And yes, of course, the pros are really cons.

"Benefits" of Use

First, let's look at the "benefits" of our use:

- escaping problems
- stress relief/relaxation
- increased creativity
- enjoyment of ritual
- contemplation/introspection
- sense of belonging/fitting in

1) Escapism

It *feels* good to be high and to find temporary respite from our problems, such as a bad relationship, a bad job, or a bad life path. Instead of confronting issues and taking action, it is easier to get high and avoid them. Unfortunately, our problems will still be waiting for us when we sober up; in this sense, escapism is a form of procrastination.

Leaving our problems until tomorrow leads us to two serious negative long-term consequences. First, as the problem is ignored, it usually gets worse. Secondly, our procrastination severely damages our confidence and self-esteem.

By ignoring our problems by getting high, we gradually erode our self-worth, Eventually, we become full of self-loathing and have a complete lack of confidence. We then become trapped in a vicious circle of escape and denial: we continue smoking to escape our problems, and we then deny that we have a problem in the first place. All the while, under the surface, those problems continue to chip away at us, until we find one day that getting high is the only way to feel ok again.

When we always take the easy way out – avoiding problems, rather than solving them – we never get to feel the wonderful sense of pride, accomplishment, and self-reliance that comes by overcoming problems. Sure, it takes longer, and it's much more difficult, but the feeling at the end is *absolutely* worth it.

2) Stress Relief/Relaxation

Most of us, whether we admit it or not, use cannabis as stress relief. The problem with this is simple: it is temporary. The only way we can continue to feel the relief is to continue getting high. This leads to heavy, near-constant use, which brings troubling consequences.

This artificial sense of calm makes the brain less sensitive to natural stimulation (see chapter 3). This means that when you aren't high, you are less sensitive to pleasure and feeling good, causing you to experience depression.

3) Increased Creativity

Many creative people – such as writers, artists, and musicians – see cannabis as an indispensable part of their creative identity, and of the creative process. After all, some of the greatest music ever composed was done so by self-proclaimed weed-lovers, right?

Here's the thing: people confuse weed for being an essential part of the creative process. Weed is never far away in music circles, which leads people to think there is a strong link between weed and creativity. However, when you revisit work composed high when you are sober, your "inspired" work often seems quite unremarkable.

The idea that weed is *required* to be at the top of your creative game is simply nonsense. For those who fear quitting will ruin their creativity, rest assured that your creative powers will return as you get sober. There is a long list of artists who have quit weed and feel much better for it – Paul McCartney, Andre 3000, Neil Young, Snoop Dog, and Lady Gaga, to name a few.

The truth is, as an addict, weed doesn't help you think creatively. All it does it make you feel okay enough to be creative in the first place. Being constantly high doesn't open any creative doors; it merely makes you feel ok enough to be able to function.

4) Enjoyment of Ritual

The enjoyment of ritual is perhaps the only benefit that is somewhat legitimate. As human beings, we enjoy rituals. We like the sense of control and comfort they give us in an inherently chaotic universe. However, there are many other ritualistic activities that we can enjoy in place of our cannabis habit, ones without horrible side effects (see chapter 6).

5) Contemplation/Introspection

Cannabis use can certainly be useful for seeing more deeply into things. This is, however, a double-edged sword.

Without a doubt, *sometimes* the perspective gained from being high can offer us insights and moments of clarity. Nonetheless, this is often delusional. Our thoughts aren't that profound, our creative endeavours aren't that inspired, and our abstract associations between ideas aren't genius – they are disjointed stoner nonsense.

Granted, the contemplative nature of being high *can* be good. However, heavy use often leads to being *too* introspective, causing you to over-analyse everything and end up living in your own head. You may be so used to this that you have lost awareness of what it is like to have a healthier balance between introspection and living within the world around you.

You may even believe that "high" thinking is better than sober thinking, forgetting the astonishing cognitive abilities of a *sober* mind.

6) Social Acceptance

The benefit of stoner companionship is another illusion. The many drawbacks of our use outweigh the small sense of connection we feel from our shared dependence on cannabis with our smoking friends.

Don't base your social life on a destructive drug habit. Our cannabis use may enable us to identify and fit in with fellow smokers, however, given all the costs of our use, this is an empty benefit. There are many other ways to find connection and social acceptance. What do non-smokers do? They meet new people, join sports clubs, and take up new hobbies.

Costs of Weed Use

Now that we have been honest about the "benefits" of our cannabis use, we will turn our attention to the long list of potential costs. You may identify with some of the following:

- depression
- anxiety
- stunted emotional maturity
- brain fog (inability to concentrate/memory problems)
- low motivation
- low energy/fatigue
- financial cost
- health and dietary problems
- procrastination

1) Depression

In the short term, cannabis can ease symptoms of depression – this is why many of us smoke so much in the first place. Whilst weed may help to numb your inner pain, excessive use also numbs your ability to experience pleasure in everyday activities.

As our dependency on cannabis increases, we end up withdrawing from the outside world. Our lives increasingly revolve around our cannabis use. We stop seeing friends or family as often. Everything becomes secondary to getting baked.

As human beings, we genuinely need social interaction to survive, which is why withdrawing from the world is so bad for our mental health. As your social needs go unmet, you end up getting stuck in negative thought patterns. You start to feel you are different from everyone else, and you start to see the negative in everything.

In the long term, it's a vicious cycle: the further you withdraw into yourself, the more you rely on weed to keep yourself numbed to your deteriorating situation. Your depression slowly worsens as the damage to your brain's reward system accumulates, and the root causes of your depression go unaddressed.

2) Anxiety

There are significant links between cannabis use and anxiety disorders. You may use cannabis to self-medicate for anxiety, but in the long term it often makes it worse. It can cause anxiety, paranoid thinking, and even panic attacks. You may have become so used to low to moderate anxiety, that you think it's normal.

- Do you often feel a sense of dread – like something feels wrong, but you can't put your finger on it?
- Do you often feel disconnected from the world around you? Like it isn't real?
- Are you often restless or on edge?
- Do you often feel that something might go wrong at any moment?

If so, you are probably experiencing anxiety. You might be anxious all the time, you might notice increased anxiety after smoking, or you might experience it if you go a day or two without smoking. Social anxiety is also very common amongst heavy users, who find themselves unable to look people in the eye or make conversation when high.

3) Stunted Emotional Maturity

Perhaps one of the most damaging long-term effects of cannabis addiction is under-developed emotional maturity. At first, this might be hard to accept.

By using cannabis to escape personal problems and the pressures of life, we never develop the ability to handle our emotions. We end up using cannabis as an emotional crutch.

- Don't like your job? Smoke up.
- Don't have a job? Grab the bong.
- Feel pressured by the responsibilities of adulthood? Reach for your bag.
- Feel like your life is going nowhere? Roll a joint.

- Have relationship problems? Get your pipe.
- Feeling lonely? Never been in a relationship? Give your dealer a call.
- Feel that existence is pointless? Grab some weed and smoke that feeling away.

Instead of learning to manage our feelings and tackling our problems head-on, we distract ourselves by getting high. This leads to a vicious cycle of compulsive weed use: as we avoid our emotions and our problems fester, there is an even greater drive to distract ourselves from the consequences.

4) Brain Fog

Brain fog refers to the clouded thinking every stoner is familiar with: difficulty concentrating, difficulty articulating your thoughts, forgetfulness, and a general slowness of mind. It is the haze that descends over your life.

Brain fog makes simple tasks incredibly time-consuming, mentally draining, or even impossible. Writing a single email feels like writing a novel; delivering a simple presentation feels like you are addressing world-leading scientists on the complexities of jet propulsion. You find yourself forgetting important appointments, meetings, names, faces, movies, and experiences.

This is a seriously debilitating part of addiction: as you find yourself unable to complete simple tasks or navigate simple conversations, your confidence plummets, keeping you stuck in the addictive cycle.

We tell ourselves that weed opens up our thoughts; however, in the long term, it has the opposite effect: it retards our minds and narrows our horizons, leaving us barely able to string a sentence together.

5) Low Motivation

Motivation is the force that drives behaviour. Cannabis addiction has profound effects on your motivation: from the big – your life goals or getting your dream job – to the small, like emptying the bin or brushing your teeth.

When your brain is used to the easy, powerful, instant gratification of weed, you automatically lose interest in other activities. The science behind this will be explored in detail in the next chapter, but essentially cannabis makes everything else seem boring and trivial.

As you gradually limit your activities to sleeping, working, eating, and smoking, your motivation dwindles. You lose faith in your ability to get things done, and you gradually lose your zest and confidence. This increasing sense of powerlessness reinforces your addiction.

6) Fatigue / Low Energy

As well as brain fog, heavy cannabis use causes physical tiredness and lethargy.

Cannabis interferes with your brain's melatonin production – the hormone that regulates sleep and wakefulness. As a result, your energy levels, sleep quality and sleep length are compromised. Plus, the carbon monoxide from smoking makes your body less efficient at transporting oxygen to your brain and muscles.

The combination of low energy and low motivation means you rarely have the inclination to get anything done, and when you do, you don't have the energy to do it. You may have become so used to fatigue that you consider your current energy levels to be "normal." This aspect of weed addiction has a huge impact on your well-being. When tiredness is your default state, life is a struggle.

7) Money

Where do you think you'd be right now, financially, without your money being drained away by your weed habit? How would your life be different?

An eighth a week, a relatively moderate amount, would cost you around £100/month and over £1000/year. As a heavy smoker, you may get through an eighth a day: over £100/week, and over £5000 a year.

So essentially, depending on where you fall on the usage spectrum, you have been spending between £1000-5000 a year, for however many years you have been smoking.

- If you've been smoking for 1 year, you've spent between £1000 and £5000.
- If you've been smoking for 3 years, you've spent between £3000 and £15,000.

- If you've been smoking for 5 years, you've spent between £5000 and £25,000.
- If you've been smoking for 10 years, you've spent between £10,000 and £50,000.

Whilst it's no secret that a heavy cannabis habit isn't cheap, you may be surprised by just how much money your destructive habit has claimed and what that money represents. You could have bought a car, put the money towards a deposit for a house, gotten out of debt, travelled the world, attended further education, or saved for your future.

Money brings with it opportunities and choices. Don't let cannabis leech away your ability to fund a healthier and happier life.

8) Health

Let's not kid ourselves: cannabis addiction is severely damaging to your health.

Inhaling burnt plant matter is not good for you. Smoking irritates the lungs, with heavy users often experiencing an ongoing cough. Smokers are also more susceptible to colds and chest infections.

Smoking also inevitably leads to the munchies. Binging on sugary, high-fat, processed food leaves you feeling bloated and lethargic. Coupled with the sedentary lifestyle of smoking, eating junk food also leads to increased chances of circulatory problems like heart disease and strokes.

Stop taking your body for granted. Your future self will be forever grateful.

9) Procrastination

For many of us, our cannabis use is closely tied to our tendency to procrastinate. When we have the choice between getting something done or getting high, we almost always choose the latter.

Applying for a career-changing course, quitting your horrible job, ending a dead-end relationship – whatever it is, weed helps you put up with a bad situation and delay taking action.

Even putting off everyday tasks causes you more damage than you think. Leaving things like bathing, cleaning, or taking care of your personal appearance might not seem that significant, but it trains you to be passive and lazy. After all, if you cannot take care of the little things, how can you expect to take care of the big things?

Weed is the ultimate tool of the procrastinator: once we are high, everything else can wait until tomorrow.

Conclusion

Let's be clear: **your cannabis addiction is profoundly damaging**. The negative consequences are numerous, far-reaching, and self-perpetuating – far outweighing any perceived benefits.

In effect, we are paying good money to feel tired, depressed, detached, unmotivated, anxious, and paranoid. For the sake of brief, intermittent moments of superficial peace, we pay a heavy price. Life has become about avoiding pain, rather than seeking happiness.

Nonetheless, as overwhelming as the reality of our addiction may feel, it is strangely liberating to realise the true cost of our use. We can now accept the fact that it's just not worth smoking anymore. Cannabis, which we thought was our friend, has actually been causing us great harm. Overcoming this deception is a key part of breaking the hold cannabis has over our lives.

Chapter 3: The Science of Cannabis Addiction

"Your actions can only be as noble as your thoughts. Your thoughts can only be as noble as your understanding."

George Samuel Clason

If you want to overcome your addiction, it is important to understand how long-term cannabis use affects your brain. By understanding how cannabis alters your brain chemistry, and the wide-ranging impact this has on your body, the decision to quit should become much clearer.

In this chapter, we will first define addiction from a medical perspective. We shall then explore how cannabis impacts the brain's reward system, looking at the role of the most significant neurotransmitter, dopamine, and how it is affected by cannabis abuse. Next, we will consider why, biologically, cannabis is so appealing. Lastly, we will look at the consequences of a damaged reward system. This will help explain many of the negative symptoms that cannabis addiction brings, from lethargy and brain fog, to memory problems and lack of motivation.

Defining Addiction

Addiction is a primary, chronic disease of brain reward, motivation, memory, and related circuitry. Dysfunction in these circuits leads to characteristic biological, psychological, social, and spiritual manifestations. This is reflected in an individual pathologically pursuing reward and/or relief by substance use and other behaviours.

American Society of Addiction Medicine

In other words, addiction causes damage to our brain's reward circuit. This leads to familiar symptoms: biological problems, like fatigue and the inability to concentrate; psychological problems, like anxiety and depression; social problems, like increased social awkwardness and introversion; and spiritual problems, like low self-esteem and existential angst. Addiction results in the compulsive drive to use the substance, despite the clear negative consequences of use.

From a certain perspective, this definition is somewhat liberating: cannabis addiction is the hidden cause behind problems in your life that you may not have realised were connected to your addiction. Those problems are **not** due to personal weakness, but due to the damage inflicted on your brain's reward system.

Your Brain's Reward System

The "reward system" refers to the parts of the brain responsible for reward and motivation. The reward system includes many parts of the brain that perform various important functions:

- the amygdala, which affects emotions, fear and anxiety
- the basal ganglia, which affects movement
- the cerebellum, which affects motor coordination and balance
- the hippocampus, which affects learning
- the hypothalamus, which affects eating and sexual behaviour
- the neocortex, which affects thinking and feeling
- the nucleus accumbens, which affects motivation and reward

The main purpose of the brain's reward system is to reward and reinforce behaviour essential to our survival, such as seeking food, water, sex, social interactions, and so on. The pursuit of these things releases dopamine, a neurotransmitter, which motivates us to repeat associated behaviours.

Neurotransmitters are the chemical messengers of the brain. Widely regarded as the "motivation" chemical, dopamine functions to create feelings of pleasure. It is a particularly special neurotransmitter, as it affects so many different aspects of our lives: it regulates our moods and our ability to focus, and it affects memory, appetite, sleep, motivation, attention, and learning.

How Cannabis Works

When ingested, THC binds to the *endocannabinoid* receptors in the brain. The endocannabinoid system is a neural communication network, playing a crucial role in the nervous system's normal functioning. THC is very similar to the naturally occurring neurotransmitter anandamide, which is why it can attach itself to the endocannabinoid (CB_1 and CB_2) receptors in your brain.

THC works by stimulating your reward circuit, affecting the production of key neurotransmitters. It provides a flood of dopamine, giving that feeling of euphoria, as well as all the other effects we associate with being high.

The hippocampus then lays down memories of this pleasurable euphoria, and the amygdala creates a conditioned response to stimuli – like the smell or thought of weed – that makes you crave using it. Consistent, heavy use strengthens these neural pathways, which is how addiction lays its roots.

Frying Your Reward Circuitry

All drugs, from nicotine to heroin, hijack your reward system. The dopamine release from drugs creates a dopamine surge 2 to 10 times more powerful than any natural reward would. Natural rewards would be those pleasant feelings you get from socialising, hard work, eating well, and making progress in your career or dreams. Repeated overstimulation of your reward circuitry causes it to adapt.

The wonderful feelings you get from natural rewards now seem bland and boring – as far as your brain is concerned, why bother working hard for those relatively modest rewards, when you can instantly receive the powerful dopamine high that cannabis provides? As a result, we lose interest in healthier, natural activities, and we begin to rely on cannabis to deal with the mounting problems caused by neglecting our personal lives.

This shortcut to pleasure has a major neurological consequence: **dopamine deregulation.** To counter the continual flood of dopamine, the brain reduces the number of dopamine receptors, so it doesn't get overwhelmed by all the dopamine floating around. This process – called "blunting" – results in decreased motivation, impaired memory, mood swings, and a host of other problems.

These effects were brilliantly illustrated by a study conducted by Nora D. Volkow. In the experiment, cannabis users were given methylphenidate (aka Ritalin) alongside non-users. The stimulant provided a huge increase in dopamine. Interestingly, both groups received the dopamine boost; however, whereas the non-users reported an increased heart rate, felt restless, and stimulated, the heavy cannabis users barely experienced any effects of the Ritalin – evidence of a blunted reward system. Volkow was so surprised by this that she double-checked the drug hadn't passed its expiry date.

The frying of your reward circuitry – the reduction in sensitivity to dopamine – manifests itself in a variety of negative ways. Here is a list of potential symptoms of low levels of dopamine, many of which will sound familiar:

- Fatigue
- Anhedonia (inability to feel pleasure)
- Lack of motivation and drive
- Insomnia
- Inability to concentrate
- Anxiety
- Emotional numbness
- Social withdrawal
- Mood swings
- Forgetfulness
- Depression
- Indecisiveness
- Craving for stimulants
- Craving for sugar/saturated fats

Reading that list may be a real revelation. The effect cannabis has on our reward system is massive. This is the price we have paid for the years of heavy use.

Interfering with your brain's neurotransmitter levels should be taken *very* seriously. Damaging your reward system severely restricts your ability to function in day-to-day life, and it can contribute to mental health problems such as depression and anxiety.

Cheating Your Reward System

Biologically, cannabis is a *supernormal stimulus* – as are all drugs.

A supernormal stimulus, or superstimulus, is an exaggerated version of something that naturally stimulates us – things like food, sexual attraction, romance, territoriality, and defence. Superstimuli are potentially addictive, as they induce incredibly strong neurochemical responses.

In nature, there are some interesting examples of animals being powerfully drawn to superstimuli. In the 1950s, a biologist called Niko Tinbergen found that most birds preferred plastic, oversized dummy eggs with more exaggerated markings over their own. Some would try to sit on fake eggs so large they kept falling off. Territorial sticklebacks would attack red wooden floats more viciously than real invading sticklebacks that were a lighter shade of red. Moths are hardwired to navigate at a constant angle to a distant light source – the Moon. When presented with a brighter, artificial light source, they are instinctively drawn towards it.

Humans are no different: we are just as easily drawn to overly potent stimuli. We may laugh at the "silly" animals, but we are just as easily fooled – and addicted – to our own specific superstimuli. Examples include junk food, television, video games, drugs, pornography, and gambling. Junk food is an exaggeration of our natural craving for sugar and salt, whilst pornography hijacks our impulse towards sex and intimacy.

For all of humanity's progress, biologically, we are still just as vulnerable as the moth. Similar to the moth who dies in pursuit of an electric light, as addicts, we are powerfully drawn towards cannabis, despite the deep damage it causes. Chronic use has rewired our brains to find cannabis irresistible. Just like the moth is unable to resist bright lights, we are unable to resist the allure of getting high.

The Dangers of On-Demand Mood Alteration

In the 1950s, psychologists James Olds and Peter Milner conducted a series of experiments on rats, accidentally discovering the brain's reward centre. They implanted electrodes into the rats' brains and hooked up a lever that when pressed would provide direct stimulation.

The stimulation directly activated the rats' pleasure centre and they kept coming back for more. The pleasure was far more powerful than any naturally-occurring stimulus could offer. The rats ended up pressing the lever up to 7,000 times an hour to directly stimulate their reward system.

It gets even more interesting: further experiments showed that rats preferred to stimulate their pleasure circuits via the lever, even when thirsty or hungry and there was food and drink readily available. They even preferred it to a female rat in season and even endured electric shocks to get to it.

The lessons here are clear: firstly, cannabis is the equivalent of our self-stimulating lever: despite the pain it causes us, we find ourselves unable to resist its allure. Secondly, the reason we struggle with cannabis is not because we are weak-willed. It is because our brains are naturally hard-wired to seek out pleasure, and cannabis hijacks that impulse.

Conclusion

When used excessively, cannabis use leads to structural changes in the brain, with subtle yet profound changes to your personality and behaviour. You may be surprised or alarmed by this. However, don't panic. The damage is completely reversible.

Once you understand how cannabis addiction affects your brain, there is no turning back. **Damaging your reward system is seriously detrimental to your well-being.** Years of cannabis abuse have overloaded your reward circuitry and caused significant damage across many aspects of your life. This is a cold, hard fact that you can no longer deny. It is time to treat your brain – and yourself – with more compassion and respect.

You don't want to look back on your life, only to realise you were held back by the human equivalent of a bright light.

Chapter 4: The Psychology of Addiction

"At first, addiction is maintained by pleasure, but the intensity of this pleasure gradually diminishes, and the addiction is then maintained by the avoidance of pain."

Frank Tallis

Why are we so drawn to weed in the first place? Why do we continue to smoke even when we want to stop? Why are some people addicted to cannabis, whilst others have no trouble moderating their use?

Having looked at the physiology of cannabis addiction on the body and brain, it is time to explore the deeper psychological motivations at play.

In this chapter, we aim to understand the root causes behind our addiction. We will begin by exploring what our cannabis abuse represents, considering its role as an emotional crutch. Next, we'll consider addiction in relation to other self-destructive behaviours and attitudes you may have. We will then reflect on the possible origins of addiction within our childhood and adolescent years. The final part of the chapter will identify other contributing forces that motivate us to continue smoking, such.

What Addiction Represents

Cannabis addiction is a symptom, often part of a broader pattern of self-neglect. The broad, underlying factor behind addiction is **the inability to deal with negative emotions**.

Self-regulation is the ability to handle your emotions and behaviour. Self-regulation is the ability to act in your long-term best interests, responding to your emotions in healthy, positive ways. It is the ability to accept and tolerate uncomfortable thoughts and feelings, instead of trying to avoid them.

Problems in this area usually develop during childhood and adolescence. This is often a result of growing up with inadequate emotional support, in an environment where emotions were something to be ignored or buried rather than accepted and acted upon. As a result, we grew up unable to process our emotions, preferring instead to distract ourselves from them. To do this, we developed a variety of avoidance behaviours and defence mechanisms.

Every time you smoked to avoid your feelings or to escape a stressful life situation – your reality – the connection in your brain between stress and avoidance was strengthened. As a result, whenever you felt stress or uncomfortable feelings, you reacted by wanting to get high. Slowly, your cannabis use became deeply ingrained as a coping mechanism.

Weed became an **emotional crutch** – something you relied on to meet or block emotional needs. In the short term, this appears to work. Weed seems to help us get through the day.

In the long term, however, we become increasingly dependent on the drug to self-medicate. As well as the root issues behind our addiction, we then have to cover up the secondary issues that have built up as a result of our addiction.

Addiction and Other Self-Destructive Behaviours

Addiction often masks or exacerbates other self-destructive behaviours. Like an iceberg, addiction represents so much more than just the substance itself. Cannabis addiction is the outward problem, but the real problems lie beneath the surface.

1) Self-handicapping

Self-handicapping (or self-sabotage) is where you subconsciously place a barrier, or handicap, in the way of your success. To avoid uncomfortable feelings of failure, inadequacy, and self-doubt, you pre-emptively disadvantage yourself. By handicapping yourself, you give yourself a built-in excuse for bad performance. Whilst this works in the short-term, in the long-term it can serve to massively hold you back in your personal, professional, and spiritual lives.

Over the years, self-handicapping can become automatic behaviour. Let's look at some examples:

- John has an important exam in the morning. He knows he should get an early night and be well-rested. Instead, he goes out partying. Hungover and tired, he takes the exam the next day. John has engineered the situation so that no matter the outcome, he will avoid feeling incompetent: if he does well in the exam, despite the handicap of being hungover and tired, he can take credit for a good performance. On the other hand, if he gets a poor result, he can attribute failure to partying and not because of a lack of ability.

- Annabelle grew up with very high expectations placed on her; she hoped for a high-powered career in medicine. However, afraid of finding out she may not be good enough, she escapes by partying, getting high, and getting by with dead-end, part-time jobs. Rather than try and fail, she can claim that she is capable but it wasn't for her. Her self-concept is preserved, but she pays the price by never becoming the doctor she dreamed of being, never managing to progress in a career deserving of her potential.

- Sam has been smoking heavily for many years. He dreams of becoming a writer, but he finds that between his day job and evenings spent high, he gets very little actual writing done. He does have some small, mostly-completed projects, but he hasn't tried publishing them. Sam has tried quitting multiple times, but he always finds himself smoking again. By continuing to smoke and sabotage his writing efforts, he never needs to find out if his writing is any good, and he will never be judged.

By sabotaging your life performance, you don't have to face up to your insecurities or ever test your self-worth. When faced with situations that could expose uncomfortable truths, self-handicapping helps you protect your self-image. Drug abuse is one of the most effective ways to self-handicap.

The root problem is the faulty belief that failing at some external task means you are a failure. If you tie your self-worth to the outcome of a task, you are more likely to avoid trying, as you want to avoid exposing yourself to possible failure. What we fail to understand is that it is okay to fail at things; it is through failure we learn. If you never make any mistakes, you never learn anything, and you never grow. The tragic irony of self-handicapping is that by avoiding the risk of failure, we end up guaranteeing failure in the long term.

Self-handicapping is one of the most common psychological drives behind addiction. If you have managed to be a "functional" stoner, imagine how well you could be doing if you took the obstacle of weed away: stop retarding your life by swimming against the current, operating at a fraction of what you are capable of.

2) Procrastination

We all know that smoking cannabis goes hand-in-hand with procrastination. Cannabis is a procrastinator's dream: you can distract yourself for hours, days, weeks, months, or even years. Few things are as effective as cannabis for enabling you to avoid jobs, responsibilities, and difficult questions or situations.

The question is, why do we procrastinate in the first place? The answer to this is varied: we may be afraid to fail (we would rather people thought we were lazy than incapable), we may be afraid of our potential, we might be afraid of success, or we might even be afraid of work. Procrastination may also be a passive form of rebellion – rebelling against controlling parents or other authority figures.

Ultimately, cannabis is all about enjoying the present moment at the expense of your future self. All the things you could accomplish today, to help get you closer to your goals and improve your mind and body, remain undone; everything is postponed to some random point in the future, one that never comes.

3) Perfectionism

Perfectionism is procrastination's best friend, both of which contribute to depression.

At its extreme, perfectionism is a debilitating behaviour. If you demand perfection in your endeavours, you will usually end up doing nothing, since the amount of work and stress involved in making something perfect – a song, a book, an essay, a job, whatever it may be – is so great that the task seems insurmountable. Instead, you opt to do nothing: the higher the stakes, the greater the fear of failure.

If you are terrified of making mistakes, thinking that everything has to be perfect, you will likely procrastinate, and getting high is an excellent distraction. A vicious cycle ensues: you use weed to distract yourself from the anxiety and depression you have developed due to the lack of progress you have made in your life, due to the perpetual cycle of procrastination and weed use. This is what keeps people trapped in the cycle of addiction for years.

4) Learned Helplessness

Learned helplessness is about feeling out of control over your fate – something all addicts are familiar with.

In 1965, a psychologist called Martin Seligman conducted an experiment. A dog was placed in a crate, and when a bell rang, it was given an electric shock. After a while, the bell rang, but it was not followed by a shock. However, the dog reacted as though there was.

In the next phase of the experiment, Seligman placed the dog in another crate, one with a divide down the middle. The dog could easily jump over the divide to the other side. Seligman gave a light shock to the side the dog was on. Even though it could easily jump to safety, it just sat there, taking it. Seligman then placed different dogs in the crate, ones that hadn't experienced the earlier shocks. Those dogs, when shocked, jumped to safety on the other side. So, even though there was an easy escape, the initial dog – that had been subjected to trauma – felt powerless to act.

Addiction makes you feel powerless to change your circumstances, even when you do actually have the power. Learned helplessness often occurs as a result of traumatic experiences, but it is also a by-product of addiction. As you try and fail to overcome your addiction, you end up feeling hopeless, worthless, and incapable of managing your life.

5) Anger Issues

Repressed anger is often another driving force behind addiction: anger over your life path, your job, your relationship, your finances, the way your parents have treated you, or just the injustices of life. Many other repressed emotions also manifest themselves as anger.

Everyone knows that weed is used to self-medicate anxiety and depression, yet it is also widely used to reduce and mask repressed anger. Indeed, the numbing aspect of weed makes it an incredibly attractive drug to those with anger issues.

As with so many aspects of weed, using it works in the short-term, but not in the long term. You may soothe your anger for the moment, but the side effects of heavy use soon outweigh those benefits, as any reader of this book will agree. You need to work on yourself: find out why you are angry and do something about it.

6) Experiential Avoidance

Experiential avoidance is the attempt to avoid uncomfortable thoughts, feelings, memories, and experiences, even when doing so is severely damaging.

This is one of the key driving forces behind our weed abuse: you smoke to forget about your problems and any distressing thoughts about your life. This behaviour quickly reinforces itself, and it soon becomes automatic, as you opt to remain in your hazy comfort zone.

Let's take an example.

Emma is a massive stoner. She has spent the last several years in a dead-end job, choosing to spend her evenings smoking and playing video games. She has been single for quite some time. Deep down, she craves a rewarding career and the intimacy and companionship of a relationship. However, due to uncomfortable feelings of inadequacy (Is she smart enough for that high-powered job? Is she attractive enough for that potential partner?) she avoids her troubling thoughts by smoking away the evenings. She occasionally hooks up with people and occasionally searches online for jobs more appropriate for her skills, but the end result is always the same: she sticks with smoking and just gets by.

What's the problem with Emma's behaviour?

Experiential avoidance is a **short-term orientated behaviour**: while you may feel temporarily better by avoiding whatever thought or feeling is making you uncomfortable, by failing to act on that feeling, you don't address the problem. This means the problem persists, and without confronting it head-on, it often festers into depression.

In the long term, experiential avoidance is profoundly damaging. As any addict knows, it takes a huge amount of time and energy to maintain an addiction. The potential experiences and personal growth that you lose every time you delay quitting is a tragedy; you end up barely scratching the surface of what life has to offer, because you are ultimately afraid to confront your fears.

The Childhood Roots of Addiction

If we are truly serious about understanding and beating weed addiction, we must look back to our childhood. There, we will discover the origins of our addiction. It is the damage done during our formative years, as children and adolescents, that increases the chance of addiction.

The emotional legacy of childhood can be difficult to come to terms with. Having known no different, many people who struggle with addiction and other mental health problems fail to make the link between their emotionally-troubled childhood and their adult problems.

The consequences of emotional trauma include the following:

lacking a sense of belonging, being out of touch with your feelings, being very hard on yourself, feeling unable to accept help, and generally feeling isolated and disconnected.

Many leading addiction experts, such as Gabor Mate, argue that it is not so much the substance itself that is addictive; rather, it is our life experiences and emotional baggage that cause us to feel the need to abuse drugs and to engage in other addictive sorts of behaviour. John Bradshaw, the highly influential counsellor and addiction expert, argued that co-dependency – where you have an unhealthy emotional relationship with one or more parents – is the foundation of addiction. It is this inner pain that drives us to need to escape our feelings.

Contemplating where our addictive tendency comes from can be painful and distressing. However, uncovering the causes removes some of the pain, as it acknowledges that our addiction is not a result of personal weakness, but of circumstance. Just like a wound needs air to heal, so too must we air out our inner emotional pain.

So, how might your childhood and past experiences have increased the likelihood of developing cannabis addiction?

- Older children may have bullied or abused you
- You may have been sexually abused
- You may have grown up in a household where showing your emotions was never done
- Perhaps you lived in a very unstable, chaotic household, with frequent arguments or fear of violence.
- A parent may have physically or emotionally abandoned you

- You may have had a lot of pressure put on you to "succeed"
- Your parents may have neglected your emotional needs, providing little or no support
- Your home life may have been chaotic and unpredictable, so you never felt safe or secure
- Your parent or caregiver may have been cold, cruel, or distant
- Your parents were physically or emotionally abusive to each other
- Your parents may have pretended everything was fine when things really weren't
- You may have been the family scapegoat, blamed and rejected by everyone else
- Your parents may have lacked healthy adult relationships of their own, using you to fill their emotional needs
- You may have experienced violence or deeply distressing events

There is a lot more to parenting than providing shelter and material goods. Growing up, we all need unconditional love and a supportive and nurturing environment. Unfortunately, parents often struggle to meet these needs, limited by the pressures of parenthood, as well as their own emotional baggage and the effects of their own childhood experiences. Circumstances outside of anyone's control often have a huge impact too: divorce, death, witnessing traumatic events, and being exposed to disturbing events can also severely impact the development of a growing mind.

Now, uncovering the reasons behind our addiction does not mean we are *blaming* our parents or avoiding responsibility. Our parents were only doing the best they could, given their own life experiences and limitations. We are not looking to escape responsibility for our addiction; we are only trying to understand its origins.

Toxic Shame

Toxic shame is the cornerstone of addiction, often resulting from childhood trauma or emotional abandonment. This is the underlying cause behind many addictions, self-destructive attitudes, and behaviours, including low self-esteem, anxiety, depression, perfectionism, and procrastination.

Healthy shame is what you feel when you fail to measure up to your own standards and values – like, for example, feeling that you did something wrong and hurt someone. Shame is an important emotion, helping us to recognise and correct poor behaviour.

Toxic shame, however, is where you feel shame to such a high degree that you end up experiencing innate feelings of worthlessness, inferiority, pessimism, and self-loathing. You feel there is something profoundly wrong with you, that you are not worthy of love or respect.

If you have an issue with toxic shame, you may regularly think the following:
- "I'm a fraud."
- "I don't deserve to be happy."
- "I'm stupid."
- "I don't like myself."
- "There's something wrong with me."

- "I'm not important."
- "I'm unattractive."
- "My feelings aren't important."

Toxic shame is a powerful driver behind addiction. It leads to constantly needing to numb and distract yourself from the pain of feeling that you are somehow inferior. Addiction not only masks shame, but as the accumulated effects of addiction take hold, we feel even more additional shame. This vicious cycle is what keeps people addicted their entire lives.

For more information on the role of shame (and family dysfunction) in addiction, and how to overcome it, see the works of John Bradshaw. Some of his lectures and talks are available on Youtube.

Healing Toxic Shame

Healing toxic shame requires you to practice self-compassion. Rather than being critical and demanding of yourself, you must learn to treat yourself with kindness, support, and patience. Instead of critical, belittling thoughts like those above, try speaking to yourself more compassionately:

- "I can do this."
- "I've had reason to struggle, but now it is time to look forward."
- "I deserve contentment and happiness, just like everybody else."
- "It's okay I messed up today. You can't win every time."
- "I'm not happy that I relapsed yesterday, but it's ok. It's just a

minor blip. I will beat this."
- "That was embarrassing! Never mind, these things happen to everyone."
- "I'm not stupid; I just made some bad decisions – as everyone does."
- "I might not like my current appearance, but it is in my power to change that."

It will take time to change your internal dialogue, but it will come with practice. The next time you catch yourself being overly harsh with yourself, replace your critical self-talk with more positive and compassionate words.

Uncovering buried emotions can be extremely unsettling. If you are struggling, strongly consider seeking the help of a therapist.

Other Contributing Factors Behind Cannabis Addiction

1) Rebellion

Weed is a symbol of rebellion and anti-establishment thinking. It is rebellion against our parents, our teachers, adulthood, society's expectations, and even our own expectations.

Perhaps you grew up in a strict, authoritarian household, where you were expected to conform to a particular way of acting or speaking. Perhaps you were never able to make your own decisions, from what to eat to even your career path. Perhaps you rebel to gain the attention you never received growing up. Whatever the motivation behind your rebellion, becoming a stoner was a great way to not conform.

2) Loneliness

Weed is a powerful distraction from the pain of loneliness.

Loneliness is not just reserved for hermits and recluses. Loneliness is something anyone can experience, regardless of how much time they spend around other people. You may feel nervous and hesitant about quitting, because without weed, you will be forced to confront your loneliness.

You may be psychologically lonely, due to trauma or abuse. You may be romantically lonely, craving the intimacy and companionship of a relationship. You may be intellectually lonely, having no one who shares your worldview, core principles, or beliefs. You may be culturally lonely, unable to identify with mainstream culture or institutions. You may be socially lonely, having no friends to spend time with.

For those who have difficulty fitting in and relating to people, stoner culture fulfils the deep need for a sense of belonging and friendship. The problem is that stoner friendship is easy and ultimately shallow. Rather than putting effort and time into building and maintaining genuine friendships, through addiction, you find instant rapport with anyone who smokes. You end up spending your time in superficial friendships, with people you would otherwise never associate with, were it not for the fact that they also get high.

3) The Need for Reward

The role of weed functioning as a reward can make it difficult to give it up. At the end of a difficult task or a long day, we feel like we deserve a reward. This is natural – human beings are reward-driven creatures after all.

However, there are *healthier* ways to do so than getting high – ways that don't upset your brain's reward system and don't have horrendous side effects. After all, occasional self-indulgence is essential: it is important to take time for yourself and to practice self-care.

Therefore, since you cannot stop seeking rewards, you must therefore change your definition of what a "reward" is. Rather than getting high, invite someone out for a coffee, visit some friends, eat out, read a book, go for a walk, play a game, enjoy a long bath.

If you are really serious about transforming your life, embrace delayed gratification. Give up small rewards now for greater rewards in the future. Visualise the long-term rewards of your actions: You might not gain anything *now* by refusing to reward your hard day's work with a smoke; however, your future self will benefit with increased confidence, sharpness, energy, and clarity. Your future self will be formed by the decisions you make today.

4) Isolation and Social Withdrawal

Why attempt to navigate social situations when you can sit at home, get high and lose yourself in passive entertainment, temporarily forgetting about your crippling loneliness? If you have depression or are otherwise socially withdrawn, cannabis helps to numb the emptiness.

However, human beings need regular social interaction. It is a fundamental need – so much so that isolation is a leading contributing factor of depression. Spending your time cocooned away in a smoky haze may temporarily shield you from your anxieties, but in the long term, your mental state is severely weakened.

The question is, what drives your isolation? Is it the pressure and responsibilities of adult life? Have you experienced significant bullying? Have you not yet found people with a similar outlook and attitude to yourself? Are you lonely, or do you find it difficult to trust and connect with people?

5) Ritual

Rituals are about trying to maintain a sense of control, order, and purpose in an otherwise chaotic world.

The ritual of cannabis includes the pickup, the anticipation, the smell, grinding up the herb, the act of rolling a joint or packing a bong, and the lighting. In a life where most things are decided for you, your smoking ritual is one thing that you can control – something that you alone are in charge of.

For some, the ritual of smoking is more enjoyable than the actual high. This illustrates the importance of ritual and the power of anticipation. It is not necessarily the effects of weed that we seek; it is the comfort and pleasure of the ritual itself. Therefore, by adopting replacement rituals (such as exercise, reading, or sport), you can reduce the significance of your weed ritual.

Conclusion

Addiction is ultimately about escaping pain. Weed is a pain reliever – an external distraction from inner pain. Beating addiction is about **uncovering our emotional pain and gaining control over our minds**.

The problem is that numbing the pain doesn't fix the real issue. Imagine if you kept experiencing intense chest pain, but instead of seeing a doctor to find and cure the problem, you just took painkillers. You might be alleviating the pain in the short term, but the disease goes untreated.

Ultimately, sobriety offers us the opportunity to regulate our emotions; this is what our addiction hides from us. We seek in highness what we can have when we are sober: calm, tranquillity, lack of feeling doubtful and negative. The paradox of addiction is that the emotional regulation we seek in cannabis becomes unobtainable as addiction sets in.

Cannabis is the ultimate emotional blanket. We use it as a tool to avoid our emotions. Instead of reflecting on where our feelings come from and how to deal with them, we prefer to withdraw and numb ourselves by getting high. Remember, emotions have a purpose, even if they may feel painful or uncomfortable. Long-term, we must approach our emotions head-on, reflect and think about them. Instead of choosing self-destructive escapism, engage with your emotions, and learn to deal with them in healthier ways.

Chapter 5: The Quitting Process

"Recovery from addiction requires hard work, a proper attitude and learning skills to stay sober, not drinking alcohol or using other drugs. Successful drug recovery or alcohol recovery involves changing attitudes, acquiring knowledge, and developing skills to meet the many challenges of sobriety."

Dennis Daley

By now, it is clear why we must quit; now we will turn our attention to *how* to quit and what the road to recovery actually looks like. For many readers who know why they must quit, but have struggled with the how, the next few chapters are for you.

This chapter provides an overview of the quitting process, so you roughly know what to expect. We will first reflect on the nature of quitting, before outlining the general stages of the quitting process. Then, we will consider why quitting is so difficult and the importance of willpower. We will finish by covering common withdrawal symptoms. The next two chapters will then look at quitting strategies and the obstacles to quitting.

Quitting Is a Process, Not a Single Event

Quitting is not a singular event. It is an ongoing process, made up of different stages and parts. You may *decide* to quit one particular day, but you cannot claim to no longer be addicted after a single weed-free week.

By viewing quitting as a singular event, you are setting yourself unrealistic expectations. False starts and backward steps do happen. Many people decide to quit, only then to go back to regular weed use a week later. They resume romanticising the positive aspects of weed, conveniently forgetting all the negative. A week/month/year goes by, until they realise they were right the first time: they are addicted to weed, and quitting is the only option.

Given this reality, it's important to remember that quitting is a *process*. Quitting, after all, is an inherently volatile experience – there are naturally many ups and downs.

One minute, we are completely committed to quitting, aware of all the benefits that await; the next minute, we feel weed is the answer to all our problems. This back-and-forth between quitting and not quitting can be exhausting. There will inevitably be setbacks. Whilst we mustn't go too easy on ourselves – too forgiving and we'll never quit – we also must not be too hard on ourselves: it is not easy to quit.

Remember, we are *resetting* our brains. That is what quitting any drug boils down to. If it were easy, we would have done it already. If you familiarise yourself with the pitfalls ahead, you'll be less likely to beat yourself up when you falter, and the road to recovery will be much smoother.

The Stages of Quitting

It is important to understand the different stages of quitting. Broadly speaking, you are either in the early, middle, or late stage of quitting. Each part brings different challenges. At first, withdrawals are your main worry; then, nostalgia and overconfidence; lastly, staying the course and staying committed to healthy living.

You may find you progress quickly and manage to quit on your first or second attempt. It's great if you can; for many though, it won't be so easy. Sometimes, you'll find yourself stuck at one stage, or going back and forth but not moving forward. Other times, you'll think you've got it beat, only to slowly slide back into everyday use.

Please note, you may not necessarily experience every stage listed below – naturally, the process varies for every individual. Nonetheless, here is the general path towards sobriety:

1) The Initial Thought

The first time we think it might not be good for us is usually just a fleeting thought, soon forgotten.

2) Increasing Doubt

Over time, that niggling feeling that weed might not be good for us continues to grow. Our denial is so strong at this stage that it can feel strange questioning our use. Even though you wonder if your use may be harmful, you don't give it much thought.

3) First Profound Revelation

"Weed is no good for me." Finally, something begins to click. For the first time, we find ourselves calmly and directly questioning our

use, more confident in our conviction that weed is no good for us – that we do genuinely need to stop.

4) Initial Quitting Attempt(s)

When we first accept that weed may not be good for us, we try to quit. With little idea of the journey ahead, things often don't end well. The first couple of attempts at quitting can be brutal: most people manage to quit only for a few days at best. Withdrawal symptoms come as a nasty surprise, pushing many back into their hazy comfort zone.

5) Denial

After you first manage a week or longer weed-free, and the initial withdrawals pass, overconfidence and denial may return in a powerful fashion.

As your mental faculties and energy start to return, it is very easy to wonder if you are cured: "I can moderate my use/It's fine, I'm obviously not addicted/I'm just one of those people who needs weed to function." You will tell yourself these, and many other lies, to justify continuing to smoke. Your frazzled brain is desperate for you to give in.

6) Return to Smoking

Having convinced yourself that weed use is somehow acceptable, you continue smoking. You convince yourself that things are fine, when they are clearly not. You confuse getting by and not being depressed as victory, when the battle has only just begun.

Remember, a functioning addict is still an addict; you might be functional, but you are still going through life with the brakes on.

This stage trips a lot of people up. You may manage to smoke moderately for a few weeks (you may or may not enjoy the experience). Gradually though, you find yourself smoking daily once again – and all the associated problems return. This phase may end up lasting for months or even years.

7) Committing to Quitting

Inevitably, time and again, the dullness, fatigue, and paranoia creep back in, and you find yourself once again a tired, depressed wreck and nearly back at the beginning of the journey.

After a point, you accept that things will never be the same again –weed will never again be that wonderful thing it used to be before you became addicted. This is the turning point. You can now clearly see that weed is an obstacle that needs removing from your life. Moreover, you start to truly *believe* it.

Unlike before, this time your conviction is much stronger. You know the weed lifestyle doesn't work for you; you know it is holding you back. This time, it is unquestionably clear that quitting is the only solution. The only question now is how long it will take.

8) Relapses

Now you are truly committed to quitting; even so, you may still slip up and catch yourself smoking again. Relapses are a common, natural part of quitting.

A minor relapse is just a small setback, where you don't enjoy it, and you happily return to quitting after a day or two of regretful haziness. A major relapse can lead you to take a few steps backwards, re-denying the problem and continuing to smoke.

Whilst relapses are clearly not good, they are nonetheless golden learning opportunities. Pay attention to how you feel when you smoke, what might have triggered you to relapse, and how you might prevent it from happening next time. Relapses will be covered in detail in chapter seven.

9) Gradual Progress

The fog starts to clear: after a few consecutive weeks of sobriety, your moods begin to level out and withdrawal symptoms (lack of appetite, difficulty sleeping, mood swings, depression, anxiety) begin to ease off. You start to notice clearer thinking, better concentration, and increased confidence.

You feel the best you've felt in a long, long time. You have more energy and start to feel more attuned to your surroundings, more sensitive to life. It is exciting to look forward to how great you are going to feel after you have been weed-free for 3 months or longer.

10) Acceptance and Sober Identity

Now that you have a long streak of being weed-free as a reference point, it is beyond obvious which life you prefer: the sober life is infinitely better than the high life.

As the first months of being weed-free go by, your sober identity becomes more firmly established. For those who had gone years without barely spending more than a week sober, this is really significant. You have finally reached the point where you are easily living life without weed – something that you could barely imagine at the beginning of the quitting process.

11) Freedom

You have firmly rooted yourself in your sober life, with new friends and hobbies, and new perspectives. You are now living a "post-weed" life.

Confident and certain, you know why you must stay quit. You have a healthy respect for cannabis and the power it holds over you. You know where that road leads. You may find that weed doesn't even tempt you anymore.

Why Quitting is Difficult

To state the obvious, if quitting were easy, we would have done it already. Addiction is a heavily reinforced habit. Habits are, by definition, hard to break.

The main reason we struggle to leave cannabis behind is because years of daily smoking has caused us to develop very strong emotional and physiological bonds to it. When we consider how long we have been smoking for, and the powerful motives behind our use, it is easy to see why some of us struggle to quit.

Chemically, our brains crave the dopamine surge cannabis delivers. The brain's reward system has been over-stimulated, with noticeable consequences. We may also be self-medicating for depression, anxiety, or other mental health issues.

Spiritually, weed has become part of our identity. It has been a daily habit for many months and years. It has been an escape – a sort of sanctuary from the responsibility and pressures of life.

Emotionally, our minds crave the sense of comfort and the emotional numbness weed provides. We have used it as a crutch to cope with our emotions, depending upon it to numb and suppress uncomfortable thoughts and realities.

Socially, we fear losing friends and a sense of belonging. We struggle to imagine life without it.

Quitting and Willpower

Contrary to the empty promises of some self-help books, quitting *does* require some willpower.

Some claim quitting is easy and doesn't require any willpower at all. These individuals are woefully uninformed about the nature of addiction and recovery and are often in denial of their own addiction.

Others over-emphasize its importance, insisting that if you haven't already managed to quit, then you aren't trying hard enough. These two views both underplay and overplay its significance.

Willpower is required, naturally – so, if you expect quitting to be easy, expect to be disappointed. Persistence is key, which requires willpower. Nonetheless, willpower alone is not enough to succeed. Ultimately, the key to quitting is replacing weed with healthier habits and hobbies (see the following chapter). Willpower is a muscle that, if overused, runs out. If you attempt to quit whilst keeping everything else in your life the same – relying on willpower alone – you will struggle. All the willpower in the world will not help you if you fail to address the root causes behind your addiction.

The Return to Reality

Having spent so much time in the hazy regions of alternative consciousness, as you quit, you will be forced back into reality.

Like a space shuttle breaking back through the atmosphere, it will be a rough and bumpy ride. Returning to reality has both a physical and psychological side. Physically, you are re-wiring your brain, re-sensitizing your numbed reward system to operate normally. Psychologically, you are learning how to deal with your emotions.

This can be an extremely unpleasant and volatile experience. Once the haze clears – after you are sober for several days or more – you will likely find yourself face-to-face with the reasons behind your heavy smoking: emotional dysfunction, anxiety, depression, an unhappy relationship, a bad career, unrealised ambition, mental health problems, or a lack of spiritual direction.

First though, you must overcome withdrawal symptoms.

Withdrawal Symptoms

Cannabis withdrawals are real, contrary to what some may claim. It is important to know what to expect, so that you don't mistake withdrawal symptoms for your normal sober state. If you believe that your experience during the first few weeks is how it normally feels to be sober, you are likely to relapse. Remember that withdrawals are only temporary – you'll feel *much* better once they have passed.

The withdrawal experience differs for every individual, in both duration and intensity. You may only experience mild symptoms, or you might find the first few weeks a real struggle. In general, most people report that the worst of their withdrawals start to subside around the two-week mark. From then on, things continue to improve as the brain slowly heals.

1) Mood swings

Experiencing erratic mood swings is common when quitting. One moment you may feel worthless, then angry; then half an hour later, calm. You could be in the depths of despair one moment, and an hour later you'll feel on top of the world. Expect to experience moderate to severe mood swings for the first few weeks. You may feel these swings over the course of a few days, or perhaps even over the course of a couple of hours.

Don't be afraid when this happens – this is a completely normal part of the withdrawal process. Be patient; it does get better. Remind yourself that this is temporary. As the weeks go by, you'll find your emotions levelling out, and you'll feel in control again.

2) Anger, Irritability, and Emotional Outbursts

Remember, emotions will come to the surface as the numbing effect of cannabis dependency wears off. Anger is one of the more common withdrawal symptoms. You may be angry at the injustices of the world, angry at your family or spouse, angry at yourself, or you may just be angry at everything.

You may find yourself crying in a public toilet, screaming and shouting as you struggle to change a pillowcase, or throwing a tantrum over some minor injustice as you go about your day. You might lash out at a friend or loved one – be ready to apologise afterwards.

When this happens, don't question your sanity or worry that you are going crazy: these emotional outbursts are a common part of the withdrawal process. All those emotions you have suppressed for so long are leaking out in potentially awkward and harmful ways.

3) Depression

Your brain will punish you for attempting to deprive it of weed. Your already insensitive dopamine receptors will be starved of dopamine, and you will almost certainly experience some degree of depression. This is when you will be sorely tested, as your brain cries out for the sweet hazy numbness. The good news is this generally only lasts a couple of weeks.

During this time, it is crucial to remember that your brain is undergoing intense changes and that your depressive thinking is a result of your chemically-imbalanced brain. Try to rationalise the irrational anxiety and depressive thoughts. Hang in there; it will eventually get better.

If your depression is particularly intense, you may wish to seek the help of a counsellor or therapist. If you are struggling with thoughts of suicide, please seek professional help. The US National Suicide Prevention Lifeline can be reached on 1-800-273-8255. In the UK, the Samaritans have a hotline – 116 123. Wherever you live, find a number you can contact in an emergency.

4) Anxiety

You will likely experience some level of anxiety when quitting. This can last for a week or two, or potentially longer. The challenges of sobriety and the fear of the unknown make quitting inherently anxiety-inducing.

This effect is increased by the temporary chemical imbalance of quitting, as your brain tries to adjust without THC. Where your brain is less sensitive to dopamine, anxiety is a natural by-product.

Individual experience will vary. You may experience low to moderate background anxiety, where you feel a general sense of dread or panic, like something bad is going to happen any moment. If you are unlucky, you may experience acute anxiety or panic attacks.

As each sober week goes by, anxiety slowly reduces. If it doesn't drastically decline after several weeks, there are deeper issues that need addressing. Again, seek help from a healthcare professional if you are feeling unable to cope.

5) Increased Brain Fog

Brain fog is a common symptom of weed abuse. You find yourself unable to think clearly, form complete sentences, remember basic information, or understand simple instructions.

When quitting, this can temporarily worsen. It can last for several weeks, coming and going in phases. This can be alarming, as you feel as though your brain has turned to mush, and you wonder if you'll ever get better.

Again, remember this is temporary. Brain fog is a temporary result of your brain's damaged reward system. Don't let it push you towards relapsing, as you will only delay the healing process.

Please note, the extent that your brain fog clears will depend on your other lifestyle habits: excessive gaming, internet surfing, and pornography use all have the same effect on your concentration and mental agility as weed addiction.

6) Self-doubt

Quitting weed may temporarily cause you severe self-doubt and indecisiveness. In these moments, weed becomes a very attractive escape.

You may find yourself doubting every decision you have ever made, wondering where you are headed in life. You may consider any decision, no matter how important or trivial, to be the wrong one. This analysis paralysis can be crippling, but try not to sweat it too much. It will pass.

Don't feel under pressure to make any decisions at this vulnerable time. This is not the time to be making big decisions, or worrying about trivial ones. Try to simply observe your thoughts and let them come and go.

7) Intense Dreams and Night Sweats

As any stoner knows, weed is a dream suppressor.

Many users experience intense, vivid dreams when quitting. Sometimes, these can really shake you up and throw off your day. All those suppressed emotions reveal themselves to you in the form of particularly weird and crazy dreams. Just try to take it easy; remember to be patient and forgiving of yourself, as your mind and body get used to trying to re-adjust to a normal operating state.

Many also report waking up in the middle of the night, drenched in sweat – don't worry, this is perfectly normal. This tends to pass within a week or two.

8) Insomnia

A lot of cannabis smokers use weed's sedative properties to help them sleep. One of the common side effects of quitting is difficulty sleeping, which can be a powerful force motivating you to relapse.

Cannabis boosts melatonin levels in the short term. Melatonin is a hormone that regulates sleep and your circadian rhythm. Since cannabis use interferes with your melatonin, quitting wreaks havoc on your sleep patterns as your body struggles to adjust.

There are lots of other alternative treatments to try, like valerian, yoga, melatonin supplements, aromatherapy, hypnosis, and CBT (cognitive behavioural therapy). Do some research or speak to your doctor. Intensive cardio in the day may help, as can eating your main meal closer to bedtime.

9) Appetite Issues

The effect of cannabis on melatonin levels also interferes with your appetite. Reduced appetite and nausea are common withdrawal symptoms, as your body adjusts to life without weed.

Lack of appetite is usually worse for the first few days, but it clears up after a week. Even if you don't feel like it, you must force yourself to eat regular, wholesome meals. You need to keep your energy and nutrient intake up to help combat withdrawals and to make quitting easier.

Conclusion

Quitting should be divided up into various stages.

The beginning part of the journey is very different from the end. Doubt, uncertainly, and withdrawal symptoms mark the beginning stages of quitting. Later on, overconfidence and complacency become the main threats.

The biggest danger is in confusing withdrawals with sobriety. Remember, how you feel in the first few weeks is *not* what sobriety feels like – it is what addiction and withdrawal symptoms feel like. Nothing will send you back to smoking faster than thinking you need weed to function.

Things will get easier as time passes. You will almost certainly feel very rough the first week or two, experiencing at least a few of the above withdrawal symptoms. If you find yourself stuck in a continuous cycle of a week or two of sobriety followed by a relapse, you are not alone. Perseverance and planning are key.

Chapter 6: Quitting Advice and Strategies

"If you fail to plan, you are planning to fail."
Benjamin Franklin

Quitting successfully requires a plan. Without a plan, you are unnecessarily prolonging your pain, as well as jeopardizing the entire quitting process. Successfully quitting requires both anticipating the pitfalls and obstacles along the way (which is what we have covered so far) and having a solid quitting plan.

This chapter outlines the best ways to maximize your quitting chances by offering advice and strategies for quitting. We will first outline the central key to quitting – habit replacement – before exploring what sort of activities are most beneficial. Then, we will consider other effective strategies and essential preventative measures, such as joining support groups and deleting dealer contacts.

New Habits, New Life

Quitting weed creates a huge hole in your life. You *must* fill this with new habits. Adopting healthy new habits is the key to overcoming addiction.

Here's the big secret: **the best way to beat your addiction is to wholeheartedly focus on building yourself a new life.**

There are two reasons for this. First, weed addiction is a symptom of a deeper dissatisfaction with life. Quitting removes the numbing effect of weed on your life, exposing you to reality – the reality you have been avoiding. This is why it is so important to build a mentally and physically healthier life by embracing new habits. **If you do nothing to change the circumstances that drive you towards weed use, relapse is almost certain.**

Secondly, quitting frees up huge amounts of time. If you are sitting around bored, sooner or later, you will start thinking about smoking, and eventually, you will convince yourself to give in. Fighting boredom drains your willpower and makes quitting much more difficult.

Beware of replacing your addiction with another addiction: if you choose to "quit" weed, but replace it with mindless internet browsing, drinking, pornography, video games, or any isolated, dopamine-intensive activity, you will slow the healing process. In the short term it can help to distract yourself, but you must make sure you get busy building a new life – otherwise you'll likely resume your cannabis use.

Recommended Activities

The following activities will not only help you battle withdrawals by keeping yourself occupied, which is half the battle, but they will also accelerate the healing of your brain's broken reward system.

As your mood, energy, and motivation slowly return to normal, you'll feel increased pleasure and joy from day-to-day life. Remember, we use weed to withdraw into ourselves and avoid the uncomfortable, so use this opportunity to start living.

1) Exercise

Many ex-addicts swear that exercise was the magic bullet that helped them beat their addiction. Exercise is an amazing antidote to addiction for several reasons: it helps alleviate withdrawals, it helps boost your mood with feel-good endorphins, and it also helps with sleep issues and appetite. Exercise will make you feel better about yourself and give you a more positive self-image; this is vital when trying to quit, as it helps improve your sense of self, which is what addiction attempts to fill.

Exercise helps to kick-start the recovery process, getting your brain and body on the right track. It becomes a great new habit to focus on, taking up afternoons or evenings you would otherwise be sitting around, fighting temptations to smoke. Whereas drug abuse is ultimately a sign of self-neglect, exercise represents self-care and the placement of long-term growth over short-term pleasure.

Join a gym; join a yoga, tai chi, or martial arts class; take up swimming, cycling, or running; get some free weights or home-gym equipment – whatever you feel most comfortable with.

2) Sport

Sport is a great way to combine the benefits of exercise and socialising. It is also great to feel the adrenaline and the thrill of competition. Most importantly, like any exercise, it helps to kick-start your exhausted reward system.

There must be at least one sport you enjoy playing or one that you showed a flair for or interest in when you were younger: football, tennis, golf, badminton, hockey, baseball, trampolining, table tennis, diving, archery, cricket, boxing, rugby, gymnastics, volleyball, basketball, netball, triathlon, rowing, lacrosse, martial arts, skiing, squash, softball, fencing, handball, snowboarding, curling, bowling, darts, water polo, skateboarding, surfing – the list goes on.

3) Meditation

Many ex-smokers report that practising meditation made quitting significantly easier. If you find yourself a little hesitant, keep an open mind. The benefits of meditation are tremendous. Meditation is about quieting your mind and finding peace, contentment, and perspective; it is about seeking internal contentment versus external pleasure, which is exactly what we seek from cannabis.

Meditation might just provide you with the emotional support that you have been seeking by getting high. It is simply a far more effective and healthier way of achieving this. Let meditation help you navigate your emotions and soothe your emotional sores.

There are many different places to get started: look on YouTube, head to your local library, join a class, buy a book, or have a look online. Headspace.com is recommended as a good place to start.

4) Creative Activities

You may already pursue a creative hobby, or perhaps you used to, but lost interest.

Creative activities are nourishing for your mind: they help you express yourself, providing therapeutic release. There is a reason some of the most creative geniuses who ever lived were terribly depressed or had other severe mental health problems: creative pursuits help you process your emotions.

Music, art, creative writing, photography, film, carpentry, dancing, comedy, songwriting, painting, drawing, graphic design, acting, sewing, knitting, crotchet, starting a business, web design – there are so many possibilities.

Even then, there are so many sub-categories within each field: you could write fiction, non-fiction, short stories, novellas, novels, essays, books, articles, screenplays; you could draw in pastel, crayon, pen, pencil, or charcoal; you could photograph landscapes, people, food, or focus on macro – the list goes on, and there is definitely a creative niche out there for you.

5) Journaling

Journaling is a fantastic way to help monitor your thoughts and moods, and to chart your progress. Writing down your thoughts and feelings is a great way to get perspective on the day-to-day ups and downs, helping you to identify patterns in your behaviour.

The purpose of journaling is to monitor how weed actually makes you feel in reality, as opposed to how you *think* it will make you feel. Journaling will help you realise that the *actual* high you experience never comes close to matching your *expectation* of getting high. You tell yourself you'll feel amazing, have profound thoughts, concentrate, and get loads of work done, when in reality, you'll end up feeling anxious and paranoid, binge-watching TV you won't remember, binge-eating junk food, and waking up the next day feeling tired and groggy.

Try keeping a basic journal where you record your feelings throughout the day.

Several times a day, at regular intervals, jot down how you are feeling, the thoughts you are having, and your general mood. Are you feeling upbeat and positive? Do you feel depressed or anxious? How do you feel in the morning vs the afternoon vs the evening? How do you feel on the days where you didn't smoke as opposed to those where you did? How do you feel after a week-long relapse? How do you feel after a day of sobriety? Two days? Three days? A week?

Writing all this down shows you, in your own words, exactly how unrewarding and pointless your cannabis addiction really is.

6) Diet and Healthy Eating

One of the kindest things you can do for yourself in general, as well as to make quitting easier, is to eat healthily.

During the healing process, certain foods should be avoided. Cut down (or even cut out) processed foods, dairy products, red meat, and refined sugar. Refined sugar is particularly troublesome: it causes dopamine spikes, disrupting your reward system in a similar way to drugs. By avoiding processed sugar, you will help your reward system recover faster. Watch out for white bread and other sugary carbohydrates. Some people even report that sugar-induced dopamine spikes can trigger relapses.

Try to eat more fruits and vegetables, and make sure you drink plenty of water (2 litres daily) to help your kidneys and liver in the detox process. Also, keep alcohol intake to a minimum – the carefree effects of alcohol can easily lead to relapse; plus, its depressant effects will not help your energy levels.

Here is a brief overview of key food groups to help you detox from weed:

- *Leafy green vegetables* – Cruciferous vegetables like broccoli, cabbage, kale, spinach, watercress, greens, and lettuce are nature's nutritional powerhouses, full of vitamins, minerals, and antioxidants.

- *Lean meats and healthy protein* – Eat leaner proteins (like chicken, fish, or meat substitutes), healthy seeds and grains (like quinoa and flaxseed), legumes (like chickpeas, beans, and lentils), eggs, and nuts. Protein is used by the body to repair cells and tissues.

- *Fruits* – Consume citrus fruits high in vitamin C (lemons, limes, and grapefruit), and fruits and berries that are relatively low in sugar and high in antioxidants (blueberries, cranberries, blackberries, strawberries, melon, peaches, and mangos). You can't really go wrong with any fruit or vegetable, but these are notable mentions.

- *Healthy fats* – Make sure to include avocados, nuts, fish high in omega-3 (salmon), and healthy oils (like grapeseed, olive, or coconut oil). These healthy fats help with brain function and mood, as well as improve nutrient absorption.

- *Miscellaneous* – Ginger tea, green tea, seaweed, spices (turmeric, chilli).

Changing your diet may be difficult at first, but it does get easier in time. As your taste buds adapt from a high-sugar and high-salt diet, fruits and vegetables will get tastier and more enjoyable. Preparing food is also calming and beneficial in itself, keeping your mind and hands occupied from thoughts of smoking.

7) Reading

Reading is food for the brain. Starve yourself of vitamin C and you'll get scurvy; starve yourself of reading and you'll be mentally malnourished.

Whatever your interest, reading is a gift to yourself. It is a form of self-care, which as cannabis addicts, we are used to neglecting. Whether you fancy an escapist fantasy, thriller or romance, deep-thinking philosophy, or practical self-improvement, there is a genre for everyone.

For a lot of people, weed interferes with the simpler pleasures. You may be too high to read a book, or perhaps you've just lost interest altogether. As a real-world, non-digital activity, reading helps your brain re-adjust to normal levels of stimulation.

8) Philosophy

Far from being a pointless, stuffy, academic pursuit, philosophy is all about learning to think rationally – something that weed addiction compromises. Many ex-addicts have found comfort and wisdom in philosophy, crediting it with giving them the strength and perspective to quit successfully.

Stoic philosophy is a good place to start: it is mainly concerned with gaining control over oneself and learning to question and manage your emotions. Seneca's *Letters from a Stoic* is highly recommended reading, as is Marcus Aurelius' *Meditations*. These books are to be read slowly and thoughtfully digested.

9) Socialise

Human beings, being the social creatures descended from apes that we are, *need* social interaction. Depression and isolation go hand-in-hand with addiction.

Whether you use weed to mask your depression or whether weed has caused it, socialising is one of the best things you can do to improve your chances of quitting, and more importantly, to improve your life.

Join a sports club, a book group, a running group, volunteer (at an old folk's home, a school, an animal shelter, a charity shop, at a company where you would love to work), reconnect with old friends, ask someone out for lunch or a drink, or try online meetup groups (like meetup.com).

For those battling depression, take it slow at first. Don't over-commit yourself, but make sure to take small steps each week into building a more sociable life. It is an investment that in the long term will significantly improve your mood and quality of life.

Essential Quitting Tips

1) Join a Support Group

Whether this is online or face-to-face, finding support is **vital to successfully quit.**

This is undoubtedly one of the single most important actions you can take. Peer support helps keep you accountable, and it also helps you gain perspective and support in what would otherwise be a very lonely struggle.

Without support, you will make things much more difficult for yourself. Face-to-face support groups, like Marijuana Anonymous in the US, are great for those who have access to them. Contact your local community centre or healthcare provider to find out if there are any addiction support groups in your area.

Online, there is a wealth of opportunity for connection and support. There are many helpful groups, although most worthy of mention is Reddit's "Leaves" community, which has over 50,000 subscribers (www.reddit.com/r/leaves). It is a wonderfully kind and supportive community; people share their experiences, struggles, and lessons they have learnt. You will find inspiration, perspective, and support from other people undergoing the same journey. Wherever you are, at the click of a button, you can instantly connect with fellow quitters.

2) Harness the Power of Momentum

Momentum in life is a wonderful thing. You may have completely forgotten what this feels like – the excitement of having something on the horizon, something big you are working towards, something you are getting closer to day-by-day.

As we have already established, one of the most powerful ways to increase your chances of success is to commit yourself to a goal – a new career, a qualification, a creative project, losing weight, or perhaps a financial goal. When you focus on a goal with easy-to-measure progress, the power of momentum has the potential to propel your life into something unrecognisable from your current situation.

Take an area of your life you have been neglecting: money, career, relationships, or personal development. Create a plan with incremental steps, and commit yourself to make small progress every day. The emphasis is on *small* steps – expect too much from yourself and you'll quickly get disillusioned with your goal, give up, and risk relapsing.

Once your reward system begins to normalise, the feeling you get from making progress *itself* becomes addictive. This is what dopamine is *supposed* to be used for – to reinforce positive behaviour. As you say no to temptation, as you conquer your cravings, you'll gain more confidence and power. This feeling is simply amazing, and it is one of the best parts of quitting.

3) Take a Holiday

If you can afford it, you might want to consider kick-starting your sobriety by taking some time away, visiting your family, or taking a trip to a place where weed is completely inaccessible. The time away will distract you and get those important first couple of weeks out of the way, and give you time and space to prepare yourself for a sober life.

4) Take Preventative Measures

• *Delete your dealer numbers*

Quitting is much easier without being able to order weed at the click of a button. The more difficult it is for you to access weed, the easier it will be to resist temptation. Do yourself a favour – if you only have one or two connections, delete their numbers. If you have friends you occasionally see, pretty much only because they hook you up, do yourself a favour and try to stay away from parties or gatherings where they are likely to be present. This may seem drastic, but for the first few weeks at least, this is a necessary precaution.

Now, if you have your dealer's number committed to memory, or they are a friend you see regularly, this won't be much use. Also, if you live in a place where weed is very easy to access, you'll have to learn to put up with temptation.

• *Throw away all your weed and paraphernalia*

It's very straightforward: it is infinitely easier to quit when you don't have any actual weed or weed-related items in your house. It is delusional to think otherwise.

The next time you relapse, or if you currently have weed, throw it away. It will send a powerful message to yourself, representing a fundamental break in your relationship with the drug. You could even have a goodbye ceremony: flush it down the toilet, throw it in a lake, bury it – whatever helps strengthen your commitment to cut your ties with cannabis. As you do this, remind yourself that weed is not the wonderful, harmless super-drug your cravings make it out to be. It is something that belongs in the past.

- *Limit your exposure to weed*

You must be prepared to limit time spent around weed-smoking friends – your life is at stake. If at your current stage, you would struggle to say no, don't see friends who smoke. Explain to them you are quitting and have no problem with them smoking, and you would like to still hang out, but for other activities.

With a pushy or difficult friend, you cannot escape, you will have to set boundaries and ask them politely to not offer it to you, or not do it around you when possible. If this is a roommate, and they are being stubborn, moving out might be the best option. Consider any move necessary if your situation so requires.

Conclusion

The importance of planning cannot be understated: **if you know what to expect and have a strategy, you will drastically increase your chance of success.**

The central point of this chapter is that you *must* change your habits and routines if you are serious about overcoming your addiction. If you don't do anything to alter the environment you are escaping from, you will inevitably be drawn back into daily smoking. Quitting will take much longer, and you'll experience a lot of unnecessary pain and difficulty along the way.

Plan ahead, eat healthily, get support, and occupy yourself with building a new life. Implement preventative measures where necessary, and practice using the emergency strategies to avoid relapse.

Chapter 7: Relapses, Obstacles, and Mental Gymnastics

"Know thy self, know thy enemy. A thousand battles, a thousand victories."

Sun Tzu

If overcoming addiction is like a war, then it is crucial to understand the enemy – your brain. Your brain will deceive you, play to your fears, and basically do everything it can to convince you to continue smoking.

This chapter is about understanding the mental obstacles and dangers that lie ahead, as well as the patterns of thinking that lead to relapse. As far as your brain is concerned, you are depriving it of its dopamine high, and it will say and do anything it can to get you to continue smoking. Therefore, it is essential to be prepared – and on constant guard – against the tricks and lies that await you.

First, we will explore relapses in detail, putting them in perspective and looking at emergency tips for avoiding them; next, we will look at the importance of triggers and how to deal with them; then we will explore the other obstacles you will encounter, such as overconfidence, loss of friendships, and boredom; lastly, we will consider the danger of questioning your decision to quit, cognitive dissonance, and the devious rationalisations your brain will offer you to persuade you to continue smoking.

The Slippery Slope of Relapse

When quitting, if you give in and smoke, you have "relapsed."

There are two kinds of relapse: minor and major.

Minor relapses are those where you smoke just a little, before going back to quitting no problem – just a small blip in multiple weeks of sobriety. Major relapses are where you continue smoking and put quitting on hold for the foreseeable future, and before you know it, another week, month, or year has passed.

Every minor relapse carries the risk of a major relapse – undoing any progress you have made and risking the entire quitting process. You think one last time won't hurt, but before you know it, a minor relapse has become a major relapse. Depression returns, as does the lethargy and brain fog.

Therefore, as soon as you smoke, you are taking a huge gamble. It is a very slippery slope from a small relapse to a full-blown major relapse – one where you spend another month to a year smoking away your time, money, and energy.

How to Approach Relapses

Relapses happen. However, every relapse is a **learning opportunity.** Each relapse reveals your relationship with weed more clearly.

The cycle starts to become familiar: the craving and giving in; the lacklustre high; the depression, paranoia, and anxiety; the panic when you begin to near the end of your supply; the shame and self-loathing once it's all over.

Relapses must be treated seriously, but you must also keep things in perspective. Although it is natural to feel guilty and ashamed, this can easily keep you trapped in a cycle of relapsing. The delicate balance is in not being too hard on yourself, but not too easy either. Remind yourself that relapsing is a result of the primitive part of your brain craving the drug, even though the rational part of your brain has decided you need to quit.

Try to pay attention to your thoughts and feelings in those moments. When you relapse, ask yourself what caused it. Were you stressed out? Feeling anxious? Bored? How did you actually feel when you were high? Did you enjoy it? Or did it feel more like relief – a distraction from your inner pain?

With the right mindset, you can use relapses to your advantage. Minor or major, all relapses have seeds of wisdom within. By paying attention to your thoughts and feelings, you gain insight into the deeper reasons behind your addiction.

If you still enjoy the relapse, then remind yourself of the long-term consequences; if you don't enjoy relapsing, the next time you are close to relapsing, remind yourself you don't actually enjoy being high.

Triggers

Triggers are things that cause you to relapse. It is important to be aware of your triggers. They may be sights, sounds, places, smells, times of day, people, or objects (such as pipes, tins, lighters); these things are deeply tied to your smoking rituals. As far as objects of association go – tins, pipes, bongs, lighters, magazines, posters – they should be discarded as soon as you become serious about quitting.

Months and years of smoking have created powerful associations in your brain, causing triggers to subconsciously make you crave a smoke. Like Pavlov's dog, you become conditioned by certain stimuli (triggers) to repeat a specific behaviour (smoking weed).

The more you smoke, the more triggers you probably have. Triggers also include stressful situations and emotional upsets, such as having a difficult day at work or having an argument with a family member.

Being mindful of these triggers is vital to quitting. For example, at work you might not think about weed all day; however, once 5 o'clock comes around, your brain is "triggered" and suddenly you can't stop thinking about getting high. Perhaps you used to love getting high relaxing in the sun. Every time it's sunny, you think, "This would be better high," and you struggle to shake the craving.

Do your best to avoid triggers as much as possible. Until you are well into cannabis sobriety, do your best to avoid people and places you associate with smoking. Don't go to your friend's smoke-filled basement; don't go to the fast-food place you always used to go to when high. Avoid travelling near your favourite smoking spots – take a different route. Be very careful meeting friends who smoke – when necessary, you might have to avoid them.

Cravings are difficult to put up with, but they will pass. Most don't normally last longer than 10 minutes. If you associate certain times of the day with smoking – morning, afternoon, evening, or night – try to immerse yourself in a project or hobby. This is why new habits are so important: replacement activities help to distract yourself from cravings. Exercise is great for this, as is socialising with new people, sports, reading, or any other activity that holds your attention for long periods.

You will be most sorely tested when you come across the smell or sight of someone else smoking. If you are going to a gig, or live in a country or state where weed is legal or decriminalised, this will be inevitable. You can stay strong in the moment, only to find yourself smoking a couple of days later. This is the most dangerous and difficult aspect of quitting to guard against, as it only takes one momentary lapse of judgement. Be as vigilant as you can, especially if you have had a stressful day or bad news.

Emergency Relapse Prevention Strategies

In the heat of the moment, impulsivity can catch you out. The following handy tips are for those moments when you are battling those heat-of-the-moment cravings and you are close to relapsing.

1) Play the tape through

"Playing the tape through" is a piece of addiction recovery wisdom.

When craving or close to relapsing, mentally play through the sequence of events if you choose to give in. It could go something like this: "I'll smoke this weed, then I'll get paranoid/lazy/anxious, then I'll spend lots of money on junk food, then I'll spend my evening on the couch in a neurotic mess, and I won't get anything done. I'll have spent money on numbing myself and postponing my recovery. I don't want to wake up tomorrow disappointed in myself, mentally slow and fatigued. It isn't worth it. I won't give in."

2) Talk to someone

Ideally, you'll have someone you can call anytime when you are feeling an intense urge. It could be an addiction counsellor, a friend, or partner.

Phone them, or meet with them, and talk your feelings through. They can help convince you to not give in by reminding you of why you are committed to quitting in the first place, as well as giving you general support and comfort. Most of all, they'll be a reminder that you are not alone in your struggle.

3) Breathing exercises

Next time an intense urge strikes, stop and count to 50. Breathe in deeply and then exhale slowly, counting each breath as you go (inhale, 1, exhale, 2, inhale, 3, exhale, 4, and so on). By shifting your attention to your breathing and focusing on counting, you can interrupt your brain's craving. By the time you have counted to fifty, the craving should have passed.

4) Distract yourself

Cravings don't normally last longer than 10 minutes. If you can distract yourself for that time, you have a good chance of beating them.

Whatever you do, don't just sit there thinking about how good you think it would be to smoke. Distract yourself by going for a walk, calling someone, going for a coffee, going to the gym, or whatever else captures your attention.

The Pink Cloud

When you have quit for a few days or a week, you may feel a surge of confidence. Perhaps you have gone a week of not smoking and you feel fantastic. *Quitting is easy,* you think...

In addiction circles, the "pink cloud" refers to the feeling of overconfidence that sometimes happens in early sobriety. You may think quitting is easy, mistaking the initial re-sensitisation and euphoria as being over and done with your addiction entirely.

This delusional state of overconfidence is dangerous, as it leaves you vulnerable to relapse when obstacles inevitably surface. It can also cause you to think you can moderate your use, quickly leading you right back to daily smoking.

Confidence is good to have, certainly. Feeling positive and capable is a great state to be in. Just be careful your guard doesn't slip when you go through a difficult patch. Addicts are not the best judges of their emotional states – don't be fooled into thinking you are cured before you have put in the work.

Obstacles to Quitting

Whilst the early stages of quitting feature physical and emotional withdrawal symptoms, in the long term, different kinds of obstacles come into play. You need to be aware of these obstacles in order to overcome them during your own quitting journey. It is the emotional impact of these obstacles that most threaten to derail your progress.

1) Loss of Friendships

It is in tough times you find out who your friends are. If you are lucky, you have solid friends who respect your decision to quit. If not, expect things to go less smoothly.

The first time you decline a joint, or let your friends know you are trying to give up weed, some of your smoking friends will likely disapprove or be uncomfortable about your news. This is a litmus test for your friendship. If they are respectful of your decision and supportive, they are true friends; if they criticize you and stop spending time with you, you know the friendship was based around smoking and mutual self-distraction.

If you put yourselves in their position, you can understand where their reaction is coming from. When you consider weed as a way of life, it is natural to feel threatened when your long-time smoking partner tells you they are quitting. To try to avoid this, make it clear you don't have anything against weed, it's just that it isn't working for you anymore. There's nothing wrong with smoking, but you think you may have a problem. Presenting your quitting decision in this way should ease the blow.

However, be prepared for some upset. No matter how respectfully and delicately you approach the subject, some will take it personally. Remember, they may be in the same position as you, only they haven't yet realised. The thing that attracts all of us towards abusing cannabis, whatever makes us more prone to abusing it, is clearly something quite common. If your friends do have a problem with you quitting, leave them to it; that is their problem, not yours.

Ultimately, it's normal for friends to grow apart as they mature at different speeds and want different things out of life. At one stage in our lives, we seek fun and entertainment above all else; as we grow, we want different things – financial security, a rewarding career, contentment, a family – things we cannot get when we spend our days high and vegetating in front of a screen. Try to welcome changing friendship dynamics as a necessary part of the quitting process.

2) Boredom

Once you quit, you free up *huge* amounts of time.

Boredom is dangerous and often leads to relapse. If you are sitting around idle, sooner or later you will start thinking about weed. It is then only a matter of time until your willpower weakens. It is so much easier to avoid relapse if you keep yourself occupied.

Consider boredom as a sign of not *knowing* what to do, rather than *having* nothing to do. There are so, so many things to do and see in this world, so many different types of hobbies and personal projects you could be undertaking.

Make sure to undertake worthwhile activities. If you aren't engaged with healthy replacement activities, you will likely return to smoking since you are still choosing distraction over self-development. Pointless, time-killing activities (like mindless internet browsing) have little benefit and can actually slow down your recovery.

3) Rosy Nostalgia

There is a very clear divide between the reality of smoking and the thought of smoking. When your brain is desperate to get its fix, it will bring forth overly-romanticised memories of past times spent high.

You may *think* getting high will be amazing: that you'll be inspired, that you'll work on your creative project, that you'll feel euphoric and great. In reality, the last ten times you smoked, you felt lethargic, anxious, stupid, and slow; you spent your day mindlessly browsing the internet, watching TV, gorging on processed food, and generally vegetating.

First, those good old days are long behind you, before your reward system was exhausted. Secondly, you were a different person back then, at a different time in your life when you likely had fewer responsibilities and fewer aspirations. Thirdly, those memories may not be accurate.

Life moves fast. When you were a teenager and felt like you had all the time in the world, getting high was fun. Now you are in a different life stage, you have drastically different goals and motivations.

Weed is not the same anymore – remember this when your brain tries to convince you that getting high will be fun.

4) Existential Crisis

Whilst quitting, withdrawal symptoms raging, you may find yourself facing a severe existential crisis.

You'll start asking yourself the big questions:

What are you doing with your life?
Where are you headed?
What do you want out of life?
What kind of person do you want to be?

These are big questions that need answering – questions you have spent the better part of your life avoiding.

Part of shedding your weed addiction involves gaining the emotional maturity to face life without a crutch, without numbing yourself and avoiding big decisions. **You must take responsibility for your life** – this is what quitting ultimately represents.

Don't expect to find the answers overnight, but know that by freeing yourself from weed, you can begin to make progress finding out the answers to those big questions. Quitting will help give you the clarity and energy to find the answers to those questions.

Do yourself the biggest favour you possibly can – remove weed and its barrier to success from your life. Give yourself the opportunity to connect with your inner self. Stop numbing your emotions and start thinking about what interests you on a fundamental level.

What is it that truly engages you? What do you want to do with your life? If you aren't sure, do something different, something new. Travel, try a new career path, volunteer with those less fortunate – whatever it is that can help give you new perspectives and thoughts.

5) Questioning Your Decision to Quit

The greatest threat to quitting is to doubt that you even should.

This is what dooms many noble quitting attempts to fail. The danger is in thinking you are now in control and can now be a casual smoker. This will inevitably lead you trickling back towards daily abuse. It might take three months or a year, but before you know it, you are right back at the beginning.

It's great when your confidence starts to return, but be careful you don't confuse your progress with thinking you can now moderate your use. You have been here many times before – and it has **never** worked. Honestly, how many times have you told yourself, "I'm only going to smoke on the weekends," before quickly returning to daily use?

Mental Gymnastics

As we established at the beginning of the chapter, we are our own worst enemy.

How many of us find ourselves desperate to finish off the bag to be free of it, only to then immediately want to pick up again? When you are high, you want to be sober; then as soon as you are sober, you crave the high, even though you *know* it will be a waste of time.

The justifications your brain offers to persuade you are endless: "You need it to sleep," "It's not like it's heroin," "You need weed to function," "You can moderate this time," "The problem isn't weed, it's you." This is your addicted brain doing everything it can to convince you to continue smoking.

We know the origins of these cravings lie in our brain's broken reward system, although they will often present themselves as thoughts, reasons, and rationalisations as to why you should get high. Even though you know cannabis is bad for you, and that you are unable to moderate, your brain does everything it can to get you to give in. The addicted part of your brain is very cunning – it will say anything it can to get its dopamine rush, regardless of the long-term pain it will cause you.

Cognitive Dissonance and Addiction

Cognitive dissonance is what keeps people addicted, trapped in a perpetual cycle of quitting and relapsing. It is the tension that results from a conflict in your beliefs. Our minds strive for harmony, so we alter our beliefs to avoid feeling uncomfortable. This is often done by doubting one of the conflicting beliefs, or minimizing the importance of it.

For example, as a cannabis smoker, you know smoking burnt plant matter is bad for you and you know it makes you lazy. But you still want to smoke it – this conflict makes you uncomfortable.

So, you justify your continued use by doubting the validity of the studies linking cannabis to lung cancer – you tell yourself it is anti-pot propaganda, and that you've never heard of any weed smoker getting cancer. You then reduce the significance of the brain fog and lethargy by reasoning it is better to live in the now, because you never know when your time is up.

List of Justifications

All these rationalisations have one goal in mind: to get you to smoke again. Take them for what they are – bad arguments based on faulty reasoning. The following justifications threaten to shift your mindset from thinking quitting is *necessary*, to thinking you can smoke weed without it negatively impacting your life.

Be on your guard and keep a watchful eye on your thoughts. In the heat of the moment, these rationalisations seem to make perfect sense, convincing you to give in. We must educate ourselves so we can recognise them when they come up, and not fall prey to them.

When they inevitably come up, you must be strong and say, "Brain, I know what you are trying to do; your reasoning might sound good, but it is nonsense. I see through your lies!"

1) "Weed is natural."

So are poisonous mushrooms, heroin, cannibalism, and murder. Just because weed is "natural" does not mean it is automatically good. This is known as the naturalistic fallacy.

2) "Weed lifts my depression."

Weed gives the illusion of curing your depression. It is, however, only a short-term fix.

The reasons behind depression are deep and complicated. All smoking does is temporarily relieve the symptoms, as in, you don't feel horrible for a few hours. Unfortunately, the only way for this to work is to smoke often. This leads to further negative side effects, as your brain's reward system deteriorates.

In the short term, quitting weed and dealing with depression is incredibly difficult. Like so many other problems it promises to solve, cannabis doesn't solve anything; it just puts it off to another day.

Weed may provide refuge from your depression in the short term, but in the long term it holds you back from managing your emotions and overcoming the black dog.

3) "It's ok to do it every once in a while. Excess is the problem; smoking a little is ok."

This sounds mighty fine, except it ignores the fact that we are unable to moderate. For a portion of weed-smokers, moderation is out of the question. We have tried countless times, but it always ends up becoming all-or-nothing. Either we smoke plenty, or we don't smoke at all.

This thought sums up the slippery slope of relapse. As an addict, moderation is a myth.

4) "But, I need it to sleep!"

Weed undoubtedly helps you fall asleep.

What starts out as a sleeping aid, however, quickly turns into a sleeping necessity. Although the sleepy qualities of weed may be beneficial, it is not worth all the other side effects of heavy weed use – lethargy, brain fog, wasted money, and wasted potential.

For an unfortunate minority who have long-standing problems sleeping that started before they smoked, quitting is more challenging.

Remember though, there are other solutions to insomnia than weed: some swear by melatonin supplements, others by cardiovascular exercise. Use quitting as an opportunity to find another solution to the problem.

5) "It's only weed – it's not heroin or meth."

This rationalisation is an easy one to deal with. Just because weed is not as bad as other heavier drugs doesn't mean it isn't harmful. It is the subtlety of weed addiction (in that you can outwardly live a "regular" life) that makes it easier to justify.

The fact there are worse alternatives doesn't mean the less bad alternative is acceptable or good. Eating a doughnut is not good for you; eating an entire chocolate cake is even worse. The fact that the doughnut is not as bad as the entire cake doesn't mean the doughnut is good for you.

6) "Weed is part of who I am."

Don't confuse your identity with a drug. You are an individual, with a distinct personality, experiences, goals, and dreams.

At first, it is difficult to untangle your identity from weed. Remember, you had a life before weed, and you will have a life after weed. As we have explored earlier in this book, we have used weed to mask our insecurities, which is precisely why we must leave it behind.

Put the bong away and re-discover who you really are. A grand adventure awaits.

7) "You just need to learn to moderate."

This variation on rejecting the need to quit and fantasizing about using weed responsibly is particularly dangerous.

This ignores the complex causes behind your addiction and implies that if you could only approach weed with the right attitude, you could moderate. It is delusional thinking. How many times have you tried to moderate your use? How many times have you said that this time will be the time you will learn to moderate?

Next time this rationalisation appears, remember what happened every other time.

8) "The problem isn't weed – it's you."

Whilst there is an element of truth to this, for those addicted, this is a misleading argument. Like some of the other justifications, this implies that we can magically overcome our addiction and use weed responsibly.

Some people can use weed responsibly with little to no trouble. **We, however, cannot**.

Weed is not bad in itself, and addiction is down to the individual rather than the substance. This is exactly the point: *we* have a problem with weed. Whether you have a genetic susceptibility to addiction, or your particular history and life experiences make you more predisposed to being addicted to cannabis, the outcome is the same: you cannot moderate. You must accept this.

Conclusion

If you relapse, do your best to learn from it. Avoid the never-ending cycle of quitting and relapsing by asking questions of yourself.

Was it complacency that got you? Was it nostalgia? Was it sleeplessness, or was it difficulty dealing with depression? If you strive to learn something from every relapse and to avoid the cycle of shame and self-hate, you will accelerate your quitting journey.

Ultimately, when you relapse, you either enjoy it or you don't. If you don't enjoy it, shake it off, and resume quitting. If you do enjoy it, tread very carefully. Remind yourself of the insidious way weed draws you back in.

Remember, it may feel good, but just because something *feels* good

doesn't mean it *is* good. It may feel good in the moment, but the descent back into addiction, with all its horrors, is *really not worth it*.

Chapter 8: The Quitting Mindset

"Watch your thoughts, they become words;
watch your words, they become actions;
watch your actions, they become habits;
watch your habits, they become character;
watch your character, for it becomes your destiny."

Frank Outlaw

The most important asset we have in our quest for cannabis sobriety is our mindset.

So far in this book, we have looked at the science and psychology of addiction; we have explored the quitting process; we have considered the obstacles; and we have covered helpful strategies and tips. The final topic concerns the way we *think* about quitting.

This chapter is all about cultivating a healthy attitude towards quitting. First, we shall establish the key aspects of the quitting mindset, before addressing the importance of having faith in yourself; we will then consider how to recognise progress; lastly, we will look at the self-limiting beliefs that may be holding us back.

The Quitting Mindset

As with everything in life, attitude is vital. Whether you succeed or fail is largely determined not by setbacks or obstacles themselves, but by how you respond to them.

Quitting cannabis will be much easier if we practice looking at things from a constructive mindset. If you are serious about quitting, embrace the following attitudes:

1) Self-Compassion

Be kind to yourself. Take care of yourself by engaging in nourishing activities.

If you mess up or relapse, don't beat yourself up. Being too tough on yourself causes a negative cycle of shame, anger and frustration that only serves to keep you stuck in the cycle of addiction. On the other hand, don't treat it like it doesn't matter! Minor relapses are not the end of the world – just make sure they don't turn into major ones.

In moments of struggle, don't shame yourself for not being good enough or not trying hard enough.

Avoid negative self-talk. Instead, acknowledge that quitting is difficult, and remind yourself that it is okay to struggle. Not everything in life can be easy; to expect otherwise is setting yourself up for frustration and disappointment. Overcoming addiction is supposed to be difficult. Think about it: if it were easy to quit, no one would be addicted in the first place.

Consider how many millions of addicts there are worldwide, stuck, completely in denial. You are entering the arena; you are stepping into the ring, ready to fight the ogre of addiction. You have the self-awareness and determination to face up to your biggest weakness – which deserves serious respect.

Stop treating yourself so harshly and start treating yourself with the kindness and compassion you deserve.

2) Acceptance

You *must* accept that weed has no longer has a place in your life. You *must* accept that you cannot control your weed use.

Failure to accept either of these truths will eventually cause you to relapse. You must also accept the damage you have done to your brain – your brain's reward system is fried. To heal your broken brain, complete abstinence from weed is required. There is no other option.

The choice is simple: either you continue to use weed, and continue a life of quiet desperation, inner emptiness, shame, and worry, never finding out your potential; or, you break free from the green prison and transform your life into something unrecognisable from your current situation – one where you are motivated, alive, and in touch with your emotions.

If you fail to accept your situation, relapse is certain, and you risk losing another year or more of your life.

3) Patience

Patience is the ability to tolerate delays, problems, and suffering without becoming frustrated or anxious.

The simple truth is that quitting takes time and recovery takes time. There will be setbacks; there will be difficulties.

Withdrawals can really test your patience. Whilst you may desperately wish your brain were healed, it will take time. It will take several weeks for your dopamine levels and other neurotransmitters to begin to return to normal levels.

Relapses can also be incredibly frustrating, but be patient with yourself and recognise the progress you have made, no matter how small. Keep your eye on the end goal.

4) Detachment

Quitting is an emotional rollercoaster. One moment, you might feel elated and confident, the next, hopeless, and empty.

It is important to try to detach yourself from the emotional turmoil and be objective with what is happening to you. Your withdrawal symptoms – whilst they feel very real – are a result of your brain trying to heal itself. They are a normal part of the quitting process. Try to make peace with them and remind yourself they will eventually pass.

Meditation is a powerful way to practice detachment. Try to passively observe your thoughts, without reacting to them. Let your thoughts flow over you, rather than getting too caught up in the drama. This is difficult, but it comes with practice.

5) Perseverance

Never give up. This is the single most important attribute to have. If you never give up, you *will* eventually succeed.

As the saying goes, it's always darkest before dawn. When life is bleak, and it feels as though you'll never conquer your addiction, keep pushing on. In the famous words of Churchill, "When you are going through hell, just keep going."

Remember, that even if it seems like you are barely making progress, under the surface, change is slowly happening. So long as you remain committed to quitting, and you are always willing to try one more time, you will make it.

The Importance of Faith

When we think of faith, we usually think of it as a stuffy, religious word of old. Faith, however, is incredibly powerful.

Faith is the belief that things will work out, even when things *seem* impossible. Throughout the quitting process, you may feel like it's never going to happen and that you are going to be stuck in the quit/relapse cycle forever.

When it feels that way, even if you don't believe it, you must keep telling yourself that things will improve, that you will feel better, and that you will ultimately succeed in quitting cannabis and achieving a better quality of life. Tell yourself this over and over. Eventually, as you make progress, you will begin to see it.

Remember, if you pledge to yourself that you will never give up, you *will* eventually make it. This is what our faith rests upon.

Recognising Progress

It is vital to recognise progress as you are making it.

During the inevitable difficulties, you may sometimes wonder if you are making any progress at all. Especially after relapsing, you might feel you'll never make it, and you might start to doubt whether you even should.

Here's the thing: when you are making a long journey, you tend to focus on how far there is to go, rather than *how far you have come*. Remember, progress is being made, whether it feels like it or not. Every day you challenge yourself to quit, but end up giving in, there is a small change. Under the surface, resentment towards weed grows, and you become a little more fed up with yourself.

Say you go 1 week without smoking and then give in to cravings, binge for a week, and then you decide to have another go at abstinence. Let's say another week goes by, but you give in at a friend's party and have a few tokes. The next day, you begin to berate yourself: "I'm never going to manage this," "I'm pathetic," "I'm an idiot."

However, self-loathing aside, you have already made significant progress. Maybe you go one month sober and then relapse hard for a month; then you are sober for 3 months, and you relapse again for another month. This is still huge progress. To go from smoking several times daily for years, to smoking less than half as frequently, is a colossal achievement.

This is why you must be careful condemning relapses as completely negative. They are bad, in that if you relapse constantly, you'll never quit. If you aim to quit completely but end up smoking much less, remind yourself of how far you have come, and look forward to the even greater benefits that await you when you do eventually manage to quit fully.

Restructuring Your Beliefs

Your beliefs – or your mental models – are the foundations of your attitude towards life.

We all hold certain assumptions about weed – assumptions we may not even realise we have. These are ideas you have either held as fact from when you first started smoking, or beliefs you have adopted along the way. When your subconscious holds on to certain beliefs, it makes quitting harder. As we try to pull away from cannabis, these hidden beliefs pull us back towards it.

You may believe weed is cool.
You may believe weed helps you be creative.
You may believe weed enhances everything.
You may believe weed cures your depression.
You may believe weed is essential for a good time.
You may believe being sober is boring.
You may believe being sober is equal to being uptight and having no fun.
You may believe quitting weed equates to depriving you of something you enjoy.
You may believe you will be able to moderate your use, and you just need one more try.

Each one of these assumptions must be challenged. Spend time reflecting on which of these beliefs you hold, and why they are completely false, or at least very misleading.

Let's consider the belief that quitting weed is depriving you of something. That resistance is caused by the faulty belief that overall, the benefits of your weed use outweigh the negatives.

Naturally, if you believe that by quitting, you are losing something good, something you deserve, of course you are going to be conflicted about giving it up. Upon reflection, however, we know that by quitting, we are not losing anything, but we are *gaining*. We are gaining clarity, energy, drive, and control over ourselves – ultimately, we are gaining a new life.

If you think being sober is boring, ask yourself why that is. Is it because reality is inherently boring, and weed is inherently amazing? No, it is because your broken reward system makes you unable to find anything stimulating without THC in your system.

How about the belief that weed is essential for a good time? We think it is essential for a good time because we are *addicted*. This belief is the addiction talking. If it were an alcoholic complaining that everything is boring without drinking, we would not hesitate in calling that person addicted. Remember, activities are enjoyable not because you are high, but because of their *own* effects. For example, watching a film might be thrilling, engaging, moving, amusing, or thought-provoking – it is these things *without* weed, not *because* of weed.

Building a New Life

Look at quitting as a fresh start, a life reset.

Quitting is not so much about quitting weed; it is about changing paths: choosing to confront your personal issues and living an emotionally and spiritually healthy life – instead of a life of shame, self-loathing, and numbness. It is about saying no to stagnating routines of distraction and self-denial, and it is about saying yes to new life experiences, self-care, self-honesty and pursuing your potential.

The best way to approach quitting is to focus on building a new life. This helps put things in perspective, giving you the strength to stay on course, avoid temptation and avoid relapses. Yes, you *could* get high right now, which may or may not feel great; however, more than anything, you want a new, better life.

Quitting is a golden opportunity. Quitting is the perfect opportunity to transform your life into what you would like it to be. You know weed is holding you back, so let it go, embrace the uncertainty, and carve out a new life for yourself.

This is the most liberating part of sobriety – you are no longer a stoner. You can completely redefine yourself. As your identity as a stoner dies, you are free to choose another one. Pick up new routines and new goals that will enable you to become a more balanced, well-rounded, physically and mentally healthier individual.

Change careers; change your appearance; try new things; join new clubs, groups or societies; volunteer; start a business. Think of all the wonderful possibilities out there and start taking steps towards your goals. The stakes are high – you only get one life.

Healthy Expectations

The journey to freedom from addiction can be long and difficult. This is not to put anyone off but to help you respect the amount of effort it is going to take to gain your freedom. Claiming quitting is easy might inspire confidence in some; however, for those who struggle, it will result in shame and feelings of inadequacy. After all, if it is easy to quit, why are you struggling?

Hopefully, you will not struggle too much. But, for those whose addiction is severe, it is important to respect the effort involved. Don't delude yourself into thinking it will be easy; this will help you stay on course.

Try to imagine just how great you will feel, how confident and amazing it will be to have conquered your greatest weakness. This may be difficult, especially if you have been smoking away and self-medicating all your problems. In this case, it is probably going to be difficult to remember what feeling good felt like. Nonetheless, try your hardest to imagine what it would feel like to feel grounded, confident, calm, motivated and energised. *This* is what we are doing this for. We are putting down the weed because it stands between our current sorry state of being and our best selves.

Once you build up some momentum, having gotten over the initial withdrawal period, you will begin noticing some positive effects.

You'll start to feel a *little* better about yourself. Each day that goes by sober adds a little bit of momentum to your life; it makes you feel just a little better. Week by week, this begins to accumulate, and then as the months slowly tick by, all of a sudden, you notice you feel *significantly better*. You might not yet be where you want to be; however, you cannot deny you feel *pretty good*, certainly the best you've felt in quite some time. This is a fantastic achievement to behold.

How Will I Know I Have Truly Quit?

As cheesy as it sounds, you will know when you have truly quit. Not only will you have a long streak of quitting under your belt, but more importantly, you will think about weed in a completely different way. You will genuinely not be interested in smoking at all, having firmly accepted that it is a profoundly harmful thing for you to do.

It is difficult to pin down a set length of time before you can officially declare yourself free from weed. However, for the sake of having a practical goal to reach, 90 days of complete abstinence is a solid target to aim for.

Will I Ever Smoke Again?

This is a pointless question to ask. Asking this question implies you still *want* to be smoking, which is a sign that you are still in the wrong mindset for quitting.

The answer is a simple "no". As far as you are concerned, when you have truly succeeded in quitting, you will have no inclination to start smoking again. You will be utterly clear on the downsides of weed use; you will accept weed as your weakness – as your kryptonite. This is the correct quitting mindset to have.

Let's be clear: **this book is about quitting weed forever – complete abstinence.**

For those who do end up smoking again far off in the future, they are often surprised by how little they enjoy it. For others, it may mean a slow descent back into addiction, with all the horrible consequences that we know all too well. It's just not worth thinking about.

Think of it as an alcoholic would – they wouldn't think that in a year or two they'll have a beer again just to see. They know their weakness, and they don't want to even invite the possibility of becoming addicted again.

Conclusion

The quitting mindset is about looking beyond the short-term, keeping your eye on the prize of sobriety.

It is acceptance of your toxic relationship with weed.
It is thinking about addiction and weed in a deeper way, considering what it represents and putting its role in your life in perspective.
It is a commitment to realising your potential, seeking something greater than weed could ever offer.

It is about having faith in the process.

It is about challenging your assumptions about weed and committing to living the weed-free life.

Chapter 9: The Motivation Chapter

"It's the repetition of affirmations that leads to belief. And once that belief becomes a deep conviction, things begin to happen."

Muhammad Ali

Quitting can be a long and meandering road. Once the worst of the withdrawals have passed, great rewards await you.

There are two purposes of this chapter: firstly, to highlight the rewards that lie ahead; secondly, to provide inspiring, concise pieces of wisdom and advice, designed to be easy to remember.

So far, we have covered the problems we have with cannabis, the difficulties in quitting, and the recovery process. Now it's time to look *forward* to the benefits that await you. You may find yourself coming back to this chapter over and over again.

It is important to embrace the future positives, rather than focusing on avoiding the negatives. That is why this section exists: we are quitting weed not just because we don't want the negative effects anymore, but we are quitting to transform our lives. Rather than relying on the negatives of our current situations to push us forward, it will be a lot easier to reach sobriety if we have something *pulling us towards it*.

For those who push through the first few weeks of sobriety, great benefits await.

The Benefits of Sobriety

1) Energy

One of the most far-reaching benefits of living the weed-free life is the amount of energy you unleash.

Having gotten used to your slow, tired way of living, you have long forgotten what having *real* energy and drive felt like. You may have never considered that weed was responsible.

Until you experience this surge in energy, you may find it hard to believe – it really is staggering. Through the combination of a new attitude, a healthier reward system, momentum, and increasing confidence, quitting weed is hugely stimulating. When you experience these things again for the first time in a long time, it feels like a new lease on life.

Other potential benefits include the ability to wake up easily and get by with less sleep. You may think that struggling to get out of bed is just who you are. However, without weed interfering with your sleep and energy levels, after a few weeks of sobriety, you may find getting up is easy – no more rushing for work or wasting half the day away in bed. Also, you'll find you need *less* sleep and feel *more* refreshed come morning. When smoking, you might get 9 or 10 hours of sleep and still feel tired; when sober, you can get by on much less and feel much livelier.

2) Time

You'll be truly astonished by how much time is unlocked when you quit. You'll feel like the day has doubled, tripled, or even quadrupled in length! It becomes obvious just how much time you used to spend finding, purchasing and thinking about weed, watching TV, mindlessly browsing the web, and generally wasting time.

Having ample time takes away huge amounts of stress and pressure that you have placed on yourself through your addiction. Managing your time better, which is something weed really interferes with, goes a *long* way to improving your general mood and confidence. Coupled with your newfound energy, it is mind-blowing how much you can accomplish in a single day – you can manage your responsibilities much more easily, which helps reduce anxiety by making you feel more in control of your life.

Time is the currency of life. Life is short – don't waste the gift of time having spent your life half-baked and glazed over.

3) Drive and Ambition

Remember, back when you were younger, when you had dreams and aspirations? Did they seem to get neglected – or even forgotten – as the months and years of smoking went on?

Do you want to change careers?
Do you want to have an impact on the world and those around you?
Do you want to embark on further study?
Do you want to start a business?
Do you want to become a freelancer?
Do you want to travel?

Do you want to volunteer your time to a social cause?
Do you want to stop living payday to payday?
Do you want to buy your own home?

Whatever your aspirations are, now is the time to quit weed, regain your sense of urgency and motivation, follow through, and achieve your goals. Whatever you would like to do with your life, commit to it, and start taking steps to make it happen.

It is a truly invigorating feeling to be working towards a goal. The excitement and joy you feel as you start living up to your potential is the complete opposite of the feeling of stagnation that is addiction. *This* is what a human being is naturally supposed to be doing – working and growing. This is why sobriety feels so good.

4) Returning Confidence and Power

One of the greatest benefits of sobriety is the returning sense of personal power. As you make decisions and get things done, you begin to feel in control of your life once again.

As you become more confident in yourself, there is a snowball effect: as you accomplish small tasks, bigger tasks become less daunting. It starts with small things, like taking care of your appearance and living space – things that, at one stage, seemed like a huge amount of effort. Then, before you know it, you find yourself doing things that months ago you would've thought impossible – like quitting your job for a better one, going back to school, travelling, or getting on top of your debt.

5) Clarity and Focus

When the brain fog clears, it might feel like you have superpowers.

At work, you no longer feel like a fraud, struggling to accomplish the most basic of tasks. You can hold a conversation without forgetting what you are talking about mid-sentence. You find your natural wit and sharpness returning. You can read a book again, without stopping after one paragraph, frustrated by your inability to understand what you just read. Your newfound ability to concentrate, recall information, and follow trains of thought is a wonderful feeling – one that motivates you to continue the quitting journey.

Additionally, you no longer feel embarrassed and ashamed by your mental sluggishness. You feel genuinely good about yourself. It's a fantastic feeling to be able to focus on work and creative projects, as well as life in general.

6) Returning Positive Emotions

It is a truly beautiful feeling when your mind begins to heal, and you start feeling positive emotions again: joy, hope, curiosity, amusement, pride, and inspiration.

The ability to feel and perceive the world unclouded by the dense fog of cannabis can be an eye-opening, spiritual experience. In many ways, it is like becoming a child again, feeling energy, enthusiasm, and a zest for life.

7) Emotional Resilience

Being free from weed brings a newfound sense of emotional strength. Given that most people who abuse cannabis use it as a tool of emotional avoidance, it is a very satisfying feeling to be solid in your mood and comfortable in your mind.

Once you get past the initial withdrawals and your moods begin to stabilise, you will become more resilient. You won't get as upset so easily and you will find yourself more able to deal with life's ups and downs.

Had a bad day? Not a big deal – no need to light up to escape the stress and worry. Got some bad news? It's ok – you'll figure it out. No need to smoke away your frustration or disappointment.

This change in mindset shows real progress.

8) Decreased Depression and Anxiety

Quitting can free you from the debilitating and crushing effects of depression and anxiety.

Imagine waking up feeling excited and engaged with life. The background anxiety and depression that has been a normal feature of your life? Gone. That constant fatigue and sense of hopelessness? Gone.

After the first few difficult weeks have passed, when symptoms may temporarily worsen, a lot of people find themselves in a much, much better place mentally. People who have quit often report reduced frequency and intensity of depressive episodes and periods of anxiety. For some, their depression and anxiety disappear altogether.

As brain fog clears, not only can you think more clearly, but that underlying sense of dread and pointlessness dissipates. As you feel less detached from life and you feel less cut off from reality and the world around you, you start to feel better in yourself.

(Please note, if your mental health problems turn out to be underlying, and after several weeks there is little sign of improvement, or if you feel seriously mentally unwell during quitting, don't hesitate to see your doctor or a mental health care professional.)

9) Improved Complexion

After a few weeks of sobriety, the bags under your eyes will have improved and your skin will be less dry. People may compliment you on looking brighter and fresher.

You'll be more responsive and emotionally available, living in the moment. Rather than a passive, sedated disposition, you'll be more engaged in the people around you. It will be noticed, whether it's by your partner, friend, boss, or random stranger.

Quitting Wisdom

The following short, powerful messages are designed to help you stay on track. Use them as anchors – thoughts to return to when you find yourself tested or in doubt of your decision to leave weed behind.

1) "Being constantly intoxicated is no way to go through life."

Constant impairment takes its toll on your life.

A "functional" stoner is exactly that – you can function, yes, but that is all. You confuse getting by with doing fine. Like the captain of a ship, you need to be clear-headed to navigate your way through life. From the energy and drive you need to get things done, to the clarity and focus you need to actually execute, weed sobriety is the medicine you have been seeking all this time.

2) "Enough is enough. I have had enough of being a slave."

Addiction is ultimately about being a slave to your impulses.

We all have impulses that we give in to. The problem is that if you make a habit of giving in to your desires, your ability to function as an adult human being is compromised.

One of the most crushing aspects of addiction is the increasing sense of powerlessness you feel as you struggle under the weight of addiction; it is a horrifying experience to feel out of control of your own life, unable to do anything about it. It is time to leave it all behind.

3) "Cannabis steals the focus from your life."

Perhaps the most subtle, damaging part of cannabis addiction is the way it steals your focus and saps your drive to do the very things that will bring you *genuine* happiness and fulfilment.

When you lose sight of your goals and stop making progress –
stuck in a state of inertia and stagnation – you become anxious
and depressed, which perpetuates the cycle of weed abuse.

Your dreams and goals remain mere ideas, unacted upon. Imagine
the pain and regret of reaching old age, regretting all the time you
spent high, the friends you never met, the project you never
started, the places you never got to see – all because you spent all
your time and money on weed, never managing to break out of the
chains of addiction.

4) "What you seek in highness can be gained by other means."

What do you seek from smoking?

Whether it's stress relief, altered thinking, companionship, a sense
of peace and calm, or perhaps euphoria, whatever the reason you
smoke, there are much healthier ways of filling that need. Read an
inspiring book, meditate, go for a hike, join a club, take a class,
travel.

Whatever benefit you think weed gives you, there is another way
to achieve it.

**5) "Cannabis provides you with a false sense of accomplishment and
peace."**

Getting high essentially tricks your brain into feeling good, even
though there is no actual reason for feeling good – it is an illusion.

Smoking releases all the feel-good chemicals in your brain that you would naturally only feel after *earning* them through work and effort. If you can receive contentment instantly, on-demand, why bother putting effort into anything?

You are living a lie – one where you feel good on the surface, but underneath you are aching in frustration and self-loathing. This is what happens when you abuse your brain's reward system. You are basing your happiness and contentment on an external source, something that has no substance and cannot be relied upon.

6) "Weed hasn't changed, but you have."

Something that can be difficult to accept is that times change, we change, and things that used to work for us, no longer do. Both in your brain chemistry and in your own character, you have changed a lot since you first started smoking.

If you have been smoking for several years, you are not the same person anymore. Someone in their late teens or early twenties may be content with getting high to pass the time, but eventually, life comes calling, and you find yourself wanting more out of life than getting baked.

Weed hasn't changed, but your response to it certainly has. It doesn't affect you in the same way anymore, and you cannot change that. These days, it only makes you tired, anxious, and paranoid. You must come to terms with this fact.

It is powerful to admit that you have changed. This important distinction helps you to process quitting on an emotional level.

7) "It's easier to keep a tiger in a cage than on a leash."

Trying to moderate is a huge waste of energy. You might manage for a week or maybe even a month, but eventually, you'll be right back to the beginning. It is far better to abstain completely than to try to moderate.

Don't make things harder for yourself by constantly tempting yourself. It is far easier to quit if you distance yourself from weed-smoking friends; it is impossible to quit if you have weed and weed paraphernalia in your house.

8) "You cannot moderate. Accept this fact."

To think that you can use weed responsibly is the greatest myth and the biggest lie of addiction.

Remember, the whole reason you are reading this book in the first place is because you know, on some level, that you are unable to moderate. This is not a moral failing. Just like alcoholics cannot drink responsibly no matter how hard they try, some people cannot control their weed use.

Don't forget the countless times you have sworn you were giving up, only to find yourself back at it a week later. Don't forget how sure you felt that you could learn to moderate, only you never did. Don't kid yourself: if you were able to moderate, you would have managed it by now.

9) "Cannabis is a sedative – it numbs you to life, whilst giving the illusion of sensitivity."

When consuming cannabis, you are effectively sedating yourself. For the seasoned addict, it does little else apart from making you feel numb and uncoordinated.

What's even worse is that weed makes you think you are having profound thoughts and revelations, when in reality, those are just brief moments of clarity, relative to the brain fog you normally experience as an addict.

10) "Learn to embrace pain, rather than running from it."

Pain is the great motivating tool of life. Pain is the symptom of our discomfort and unhappiness with ourselves and our lives. Rather than learning from it, we numb ourselves to avoid it.

The great irony is that you use weed to numb yourself to your circumstances, yet you *need* to feel that pain and discomfort to push you forward. By numbing yourself to the pains of life, you take away a key driving force to change your circumstances.

11) "You don't actually enjoy being high anymore."

Don't forget this obvious one. The next time you relapse, pay close attention to your state of mind.

The truth is, you don't actually enjoy the feeling of being high anymore. It just makes you tired, anxious, and paranoid. You think it'll be amazing, but it always ends up disappointing you.

12) "Weed is your kryptonite."

For us, weed is essentially kryptonite. Like the fictional substance, weed takes away all your power. Cannabis addiction weakens you emotionally, physically, intellectually, and spiritually; it leaves you a weakened shell of yourself.

You really don't want it in your life anymore.

13) "Sober highs are the greatest highs of all."

Being weed-free almost feels like a wonderful drug.

However, unlike real drugs, you can't get instantly high – it is not instant gratification – you *must work for it first*, then you can enjoy its wonderful powers.

There is a great secret waiting for you to discover: you have no idea of the power of sober living. Since you have no reference point (when was the last time you spent 6 months weed-free?), you have little clue of what you are missing out on. One of the greatest parts of achieving sobriety, for many people, is realising how sharp, focused and action-orientated they become. There's a reason so many top-performers proudly admit to being sober. It really is a game-changer.

14) "Your brain is your most powerful asset – take care of it."

Your brain regulates everything in your life, from the physical to the emotional and the spiritual. Stop sabotaging your life by upsetting the chemical balance in your brain. Stop sabotaging your spiritual growth by living in a permanent state of numbness.

If there was one habit that negatively affected your appetite, energy, emotions, mood, memory, sleep, confidence, self-esteem, concentration, and productivity, you would drop it in a heartbeat, wouldn't you?

Weed compromises the inner workings of your brain, which affect almost every aspect of your life. It's time to move on.

15) "Being high is an escape: using it makes me avoid being present in my own life."

In the short term, using weed to escape your problems seems like a good idea. You feel pain – which you don't *want* to feel – so you get high. The problem is, the only way to keep avoiding your problems is to keep getting high.

When you repeatedly do this, your problems remain, you stagnate, and you remain emotionally weak. Strength only comes from working through things, from tackling things head-on.

If you are smoking to avoid feeling lonely, stop smoking weed, and get outside and meet people. If you are smoking to avoid the pressures of work and adulthood, stop smoking and think about what it is about those things that you find so uncomfortable. Work on solutions to your problems, rather than avoiding them entirely. This avoidance contributes to the sense of depression and hopelessness that being a chronic weed smoker often brings.

16) "Cannabis makes me too comfortable doing nothing."

Weed reinforces the belief that pleasure is the ultimate thing to seek in life. Whilst pleasure undoubtedly *feels* great, it is temporary. The temporary nature of pleasure means weed never leaves you satisfied – you must keep chasing it.

When we focus on instant gratification, all other things become less appealing. Our desire for weed drowns out the desire to pursue healthier and more beneficial behaviours. As a result, we neglect our lives, often never getting around to all the things that we dream about doing whilst high. This danger has the potential to rob you of your life.

There are so many things that need your attention, such as your finances, health, relationships, and career. These issues end up being relegated to "someday," whilst you fool yourself into not caring.

17) "Quitting is like getting over a bad relationship."

Quitting weed is like struggling to get over a bad relationship. It has to end, but you find it difficult to accept: you romanticise the good times, forget the bad, and forget that things will never change. You may still have very strong feelings for weed. You may reminisce about the good times, but you cannot stay together based on fond memories.

You must accept that it just isn't working anymore. You have outgrown weed; it is time to move on.

18) "Look forwards, not backwards."

When we stop to consider what we have given up and the opportunities we have missed by embracing the weed lifestyle, it can be quite horrifying. As bad as it feels though, don't linger on the past, on what you have or haven't done. Instead, look forward to the future and imagine what your life would look like without weed holding you back.

Use the energy and clarity you gain from being sober to work towards a future you will be proud of. Know that one day you will look back on your current situation as a distant memory.

19) "Emotion is what makes the human experience – don't shut yourself off from life."

Don't be a robot. The foremost reason to quit – strong enough to counter the most intense, desperate cravings – is that weed blocks out your emotions.

All the good, all the bad – it's all dulled to the point that only the most joyous or sad occasions cause us to feel anything at all, if then. Deep emotions are what makes the human experience what it is. Without them, you are simply going through the motions.

If the concept of positive emotions seems strange to you, remember that it will take time to build a new life – one where you will have good things going on. Focus on building a new life, and don't be tricked by the lies depression tells you.

20) "Accept that weed cannot be a part of your new life."

Weed has no place in the new life you are building – one where you need drive and energy, clear-headedness, and a stable mental state. Getting high is completely incompatible with your goal of personal transformation.

Weed and the new you are mutually exclusive – it is one or the other.

The link between your cannabis use and your life problems is an incredibly important fact to accept: if you continue to use cannabis, you will not be able to reverse the major problems in your life. If you want your life to radically improve, you must accept that your weed addiction causes you severe physical, emotional, and spiritual damage.

21) "If you decide to never give up, one day you *will* make it."

Perseverance and faith are the two most important values to hold when quitting, and for life in general.

If you're fortunate, you'll successfully quit after the first couple of attempts. For many, it may take 5-10 tries over a period of several months; for some, it may take countless tries over a year or two. It is disheartening to relapse repeatedly. However, if you have the courage to keep on trying, no matter how many times you slip up, you will eventually make it – this is a fact.

Never give up and never give in.

22) "If I give up now, I'll soon be back to where I started. When I started, I was desperately wishing to be where I am now."

Don't undo the progress you have made so far. Remember the difficult days when you went through the first week or two of quitting? The nightmares, the insomnia, the depression, and mental anguish?

Don't let all that effort and hardship be in vain. You've done so well to get to where you are now – don't send yourself back to the beginning.

23) "Forget about what you gain from being high; remember what you lose."

Whatever you think are the benefits of getting high, these pale in comparison to the costs.

Remember not what you are going without, but what you will be giving up if you reach for that joint. You will lose your sharpness and mental clarity, you will lose your energy, you will lose self-respect, you will lose your motivation, your health, your money, and your time.

It's an easy choice.

Epilogue

Overcoming addiction is the greatest single thing you can do to improve your life. Once you commit to quitting, your life will never be the same again. If you thought getting into weed was mind-opening, prepare yourself for an even greater shift in perspective upon successfully quitting.

Ultimately, quitting weed is about solving a deeper problem – it's about re-claiming control over yourself.

It is about facing problems instead of running away from them.

It is about learning to process and handle emotions in healthy ways.

It is about being present in your own life, not being a passive observer.

It is about taking back power.

It is about not being a slave to desire.

It is about escaping the never-ending pursuit of instant gratification.

Stop choosing short-term pleasure over long-term happiness. Leave weed in your past, where it belongs.

Appendix: Recovery Experiences

Know that you are not alone in your quest to become weed-free.

This very moment, there are lots of people around the world fighting to overcome their cannabis addiction. To help gain perspective, it is useful to read the experiences of others going through the same process.

Below is a small collection of posts and comments from Reddit's "*Leaves*" community. In them you will find solidarity, advice, wisdom, and reflections of yourself. To read more accounts and experiences from fellow quitters, visit www.reddit.com/r/leaves.

1) Last night was difficult. I worked all last weekend, so I had something to focus my mind on, and I didn't want to smoke. This weekend was my first weekend off sober, and it was hard. I still have a whole slab of weed brownie in the freezer, I spent a long time thinking if it would be worth it or if it would be enjoyable.

In the end, I decided to leave it where it was and reward myself with a large white chocolate hot cocoa from Starbucks with cream and sprinkles and a marshmallow dipping thing. I sat down and played some BFL and then went to bed.

I know I still have a long way to go, but I think you must celebrate the little victories and hopefully some of the positivity will help someone else.

Sunshinestarfish

2) I knew going out last night would just make everything worse for me. I realised how little progress I've made in 3 months, and the fact that if this doesn't get better, I'm not going to form close relationships ever again. I don't even know what it is I used to do to keep a conversation going, but I need the ability again.

We're naturally social creatures, so for me to be deprived of that strips my will to live as I'm sure many of you might have heard. I'm an early onset smoker (started experimenting at 13-14, morphed to regular use right before turning 15) and sometimes I just think to myself, wow, this is nasty, did I just do permanent damage? For those just starting, I don't want to put you down though; I have made improvements in memory, quick thinking and general intelligence. I don't have any social anxiety and am starting to feel much more human again. I'm hoping last night went so bad because I had been inside all day every day for a week eating very shitty food and doing literally nothing, but doubts do come over my mind. I go onto uncommonforum and I read posts of people 9 months in saying they still have the same problems, and I just think wow, what if that's me, what if that's me in two years?

Anonymous

3) I never thought I would be able to say I would be sober a year. Drugs have been such a huge part of my life. I used various drugs from 15- 25, but weed has always been my main crutch. I remember feeling totally helpless and panicked when I would search the carpet and floors for weed crumbs; when I would run out and have a panic attack and desperately try to think of a way I could get more; when I would get that rush of getting the baggie in my hands, running up the stairs and immediately packing a bong; when I blow through my paycheck just for weed; when I would fuck random guys just to get high.

Yeah, I was a full-blown addict. I always will be. I still have my addictions (food, sex), so I still have a lot to work on. It is very frustrating to not be able to enjoy life's pleasures without it becoming an addiction. But it is not consuming me like drugs. I am aware, and I am functioning. This was by far my biggest addiction.

Life has become so different and wonderful since quitting drugs. I am more social, more focused. I'm going back to school in the fall to study psychology. I am getting a raise and a new job title this summer. I am in love and living with someone who lifts me up. I have more friends. I don't have a temper anymore. I am no longer violent. I love myself.

I know a lot of you are struggling to take that first step. I know life without weed seems absolutely terrifying; it was for me when I decided to quit. It has become your crutch and your best friend. Weed never judges you or makes you feel bad. It only makes you feel good and safe, like your wrapped in a warm blanket (pardon the cliché).

But you have to ask yourself: Does the weed own you? Is life simply impossible to live without a pipe/bong/joint in your hand? Because if it is, you need to quit.

The day I quit, I smoked the last of my weed and threw away all the paraphernalia. I could not have quit if there was any type of temptation in my house. I downloaded the app Habit Hub, which helps you keep track of how many days you've been sober. I did it without a support group, but that was just what worked for me.

What I'm trying to say is, you can do it! I believe in you. I promise you, life will get better. Each day sober has made sobriety so much easier. That first month will suck, but after that, you will feel like a brand-

new person. Don't let it own you; take control of your own life. You deserve it!

Anyways, thank you for taking the time to read this if you did. I am so proud of myself, and I find nothing wrong with saying that.

Be proud of yourself too.

Chelseamene2

4) *You know deep down inside that weed is something you have to put down. It's holding you back.*

Why pull the bandage off slowly? Why make a half-hearted attempt at quitting? Why entertain the thought that says eventually you'll be able to smoke again? It all leads to the same place. Smoking weed is a slippery slope, and I'm certain that if you've tried to quit enough times you've had it proven as such.

So, just let it go. Don't pull the bandage off slowly. Make the singular decision and vow to quit. And let it go and move on.

Of course, you really can't just let it go once and be done with it. You are going to have thoughts of weed come up at random times; you are going to have urges. But when those thoughts and feelings arise, just let those go too. Let them come, but let them go. Urges never last for more than 15 minutes, really. If you are able, just let an urge happen, and instead of fighting it or running from it, just observe it. See if you can point to what an urge feels like in your body, on a second-to-second basis. And by just watching it, you don't fuel the desire, and you can trust it will fade without a remnant left.

Powerpython

5) So, this is sad, but the reason why I can't ever seem to stop smoking is because it truly feels like weed is the only good part of my life.

I've been depressed for a while, functional now, but I don't have the zest that I see in other people. I feel ashamed for wasting all of my 20s without much to show for it, no degree, no marketable skills - my "life resume" seems embarrassingly thinner than other people's.

I don't have anyone in my life who truly cares about how I feel day-to-day (except for my therapist- she's wonderful, but somehow this doesn't seem "real"). My parents don't care, my sisters don't, what friends I have left are very surface.

It's like weed is my best friend - feel sad and lonely? Take a puff and explore all the corners of your mind. Entertain yourself. I know this isn't good for me though, pretty much every day for like 5+ years. It is probably adding to my depressed feelings. But if I get rid of it, I won't have any joy in my life, just the same old drudgery, dead-end retail job and bills and no one caring about me.

I don't know what to do.

small_kitten_friend

6) So guys, I've made it to day 6! Tomorrow will mark a week off pot and cigarettes! The first week of being sober in 10 years. I started this crap when I was 15/16.

Every aspect about my life is better. Sure, I'm craving that bowl at night time, but you can get past that; just don't dwell on that craving/thought.

This is actually my third week of quitting. I spent the first two weeks cutting down my usage immensely and then 6 days ago, I had my final bowl.

If you find yourself smoking TONNES, I suggest cutting back to one bowl or half a joint before you go to bed. Do that for a week, and after that week, say goodbye.

Show yourself you can handle day-by-day stresses and tasks sober – gain that confidence. There is no crazy rush.

I've already achieved so much since quitting and its only been 6 days. My new life is so great.

Now, if you are hit by crazy anxiety, please remember it WILL pass, if YOU face it and embrace it. Don't numb yourself to the emotional turmoil, embrace it. These thoughts, feelings and emotions are coming out because you have suppressed them for so long with cannabis and nicotine.

Learn to deal with it and it will fade away.

I thought I was going crazy on day 1 and 2. Even the build-up as I was cutting down was rough. But here I am at day 6 anxiety-free and it feels amazing. I thought it would take sooo much longer to conquer.

Speak to your partner. Be honest with your family. I told my father I was quitting pot and ciggies. I had lied to him for 10 years about being a smoker but at my weakest point, I opened up and told him. He was great about it and started calling me daily to check up on me. My mum knew and she was amazing too.

You see, guys, I have found my relationship with my family has improved since this has gone down. I'm more in touch and not paranoid about them finding out I'm stoned or smell like smoke. Living a lie is shit, and that's what I was doing.

Embrace the fear and conquer it. Life is too short!

Rose_Thug

7) *Weed killed me socially. It was crippling. Every thought that would come to mind gave me horrible anxiety that would lead me to believe any social situation would end terribly. I was awkward because I was always stuck in my stoner-headed mind. It always took me away from what was in front of me, and I hated that.*

Fast forward now, one year sober, and I went from calling myself an introvert (and to me that's just a label lazy/scared people use to avoid learning proper social skills, not always but some people) to being the person in the room who carried the vibes positively and influenced other people to follow my lead and have a good time and open up.

I'm no longer afraid of speaking my mind because I stopped caring, which made me more myself. (Believe me, self-love takes a shit ton of work.)
I even talk to more strangers a day than people I know most days because I love being out and about. Being locked in a room wishing I could be outside but too afraid to be is no longer an issue.

All it takes is envisioning yourself to be your higher self and simply executing it.

TheGreat666

8) *It completely takes away what it once gave you.*

I feel like I always hear about the benefits of smoking weed and about how it cures depression, anxiety, boosts your appetite, and so on. What people don't talk about is how after you become a daily smoker, you don't get those benefits, and it instead makes it worse. It cured my depression while I was high, then made it twice as bad sober. It cured my anxiety when I was high, then I was a nervous wreck all the time sober. It boosted my appetite while I was high, then I wouldn't even get hungry while sober. It made more creative while I was high, then it made my mind an empty void while sober. You get the point. I became so dependent on it that I couldn't function without it, and I'm glad I no longer have access to it. I just wish people wouldn't act like there are no downsides to weed.

Anonymous

I wish you the very best in your quitting journey.

Matthew Clarke
matthewclarkebook@gmail.com

(If you have found this book helpful, I would be most grateful for an Amazon review!)